Achieving Goals Through Teamwork

INTRODUCING THE SERIES

Management Action Guides consists of a series of books written in an Open Learning style which are designed to be

- user friendly
- job related

Open Learning text is written in language which is easy to understand and avoids the use of jargon that is usually a feature of management studies. The text is interactive and is interspersed with Action Point questions to encourage the reader to apply the ideas from the text to their own particular situation at work. Space has been left after each Action Point question where responses can be written.

The Management Action Guides series will appeal to people who are already employed in a supervisory or managerial position and are looking to root their practical experience within more formal management studies.

Although Management Action Guides is a series of books that cover all aspects of management education, each book is designed to be free standing and does not assume that the reader has worked through any other book in the series.

Titles in The Management Action Guides series are

Planning and Managing Change

Handling Conflict and Negotiation

Making Effective Presentations

Managing People and Employee Relations

Creating Customer Loyalty

Achieving Goals Through Teamwork

Achieving Goals Through Teamwork

MANCHESTER
O · P · E · N
LEARNING

KOGAN
PAGE

First published in 1992 as *People in Organisations* by Manchester Open Learning, Lower Hardman Street, Manchester M3 3FP

This edition published in 1993 by Kogan Page Ltd

Kogan Page Limited
120 Pentonville Road
London N1 9JN

© Manchester Open Learning, 1992, 1993.

British Library Cataloguing in Publication Data

A CIP record for this book is available from the British Library.

ISBN 0 7494 1142 2

Printed and bound in Great Britain by Biddles Ltd, Guildford and Kings Lynn

Contents

GENERAL INTRODUCTION

Customers are becoming increasingly important in the lives of most organisations as competition increases. Customers are now presented with more choice than ever before; and this represents a considerable shift of power away from producers to consumers. A number of factors have combined to bring about this change

- **Deregulation**: the withdrawal of controls and privileges which protected a number of industries from effective competition and put other industries under direct government control.

   Privatisation has been only a minor element in this change, although it has been the most visible. In the last decade road transport (both freight and passenger), financial services, air transport, radio broadcasting and telecommunications have all been opened up to competition, with or without privatisation of public corporations. This trend has been common to nearly all developed countries, regardless of the political complexion of their governments

- **Globalisation**: companies are increasingly viewing the whole world as their potential market, and pressing their governments to remove whatever barriers still exist to international trade. Many large companies have, in effect, lost their original national identities and have become completely internationalised. They are managed from a number of different centres, and produce and sell their products anywhere in the world. Competition and choice is coming from more places than ever before

- **Technology**: on the production side, modern technology has been applied in three main areas - in production processes, in the products themselves, and in communication systems. The resulting effects for the consumers have been: an increasing variety of goods to choose from, a steady reduction in the prices of what were traditionally 'luxury goods', and a greater awareness of what is available together with better access to it

- **Rising Standards**: at least for the majority of people in this country, rising real income means that a larger proportion of their income is available for them to use how they choose. Rising standards of living have led people to expect rising standards of quality and service. Typically they want better rather than more

INTRODUCTION: ACHIEVING THINGS THROUGH THE TEAM

Achieving work related goals effectively through a group or a team is a primary concern of anyone acting in a supervisory or managerial capacity. But building and motivating a team with cohesion and purpose, releasing its full potential and organising and monitoring its performance - whilst realistically taking account of the constraints upon it - is no small task. In this book we shall focus on the awareness, skills and knowledge which are the keys to doing these things effectively with any workteam.

We shall look at **motivation** in the work situation and what it means for **managing individuals**, at **how groups behave** and their dynamics and processes, at what **effective leadership** and **team building** mean and some different approaches to them. Of course there are **constraints** and limitations within which any team must work - both internal and external - and decisions must sometimes be made with incomplete knowledge or uncertain assumptions. But the supervisors and managers who achieve work goals best are those who know their teams, are aware of such problems, set **realistic objectives and targets** for success and then sensitively **monitor progress** towards them. Above all they are people who **manage themselves and their time** effectively as well as their team.

The **overall aim** of this book is that, after working through it, you will have the skills and knowledge to achieve work goals effectively through a group or team.

1 MOTIVATION, VALUES AND ATTITUDES

Managers have often been defined as people who get their work done through others. To do this they depend upon the co-operation and commitment of their people and so must be able to relate well to those people both as individuals and as groups or teams.

This task is not a simple one.

People outside work are individuals with their own values and attitudes, their own sense of what is important to them in their lives. And whatever the constraints of the workplace, they are the same people there. Their values will affect how they react and are motivated in particular situations.

ACTION POINT 1

Consider the following situation then answer the following questions.

Jane was feeling disgruntled. Things didn't seem to be turning out as she had hoped. She had left her last job, even though it was better paid and nearer home, because no one seemed to value her job skills and her initiatives were consistently ignored.

Her new workmates seemed more interested in the company and what they did, and at the interview her keenness to train on word processing and databases had been warmly received - but at the moment there were problems. Sarah Ross, her new boss, just kept piling on the work, particularly the more routine administrative aspect of her accounts. Jane was rarely told what her job responsibilities were and the pressure never let up - it was always 'Jane'll do it, if it's a rush job. It'll be right and done on time!' Which was all very well but when the job was finished, she usually got only the most cursory thanks. Now, because she did it well, other supervisors brought her similar jobs to do and Sarah seemed to think she would be happy to do it. There was not a sign of any time for her computer training.

1   What do you pick up from this of Jane's attitude to work, and of the values which will motivate her to give of her best?

2   What demotivating factors are also at work?

There are clearly a number of motivating and demotivating factors in Jane's situation related to her work values.

She is quite happy to accept a lower paid job provided that she is doing what she regards as more **interesting work** and provided she gets genuine (rather than manipulative) **appreciation** for her efforts. She likes to work in an atmosphere of **commitment** but her preference for a **properly defined role** and responsibilities is clearly not being met. Her own skills **development** is important to her but seems not to be considered by her supervisor.

It is likely though that Sarah Ross sees things very differently. As Jane does what is asked of her well, Sarah may assume that she understands exactly what her role and job are; that Jane's initial enthusiasm will be satisfied by 'keeping busy' and she will be pleased by other supervisors seeking her services; that getting rush jobs done and meeting section targets are as important to Jane as to herself; and that Jane will be happy to postpone her computer training until a time of less pressure.

What is clear is that

■ the manager doesn't see things in the same way as the employee

■ a number of unfounded assumptions about common values or goals have been made

Psychologists suggest that we all tend unconsciously to interpret what is happening around us to fit in with our own particular preconceived attitudes and values. The successful manager and motivator doesn't fall into this trap. Recognising other people's priorities and values - and **respecting** them - means that everyone can use their energies and talents together in the most productive way. Failing to see them or seeing them as 'wrong' invites division, conflict and demotivation.

CHAPTER SUMMARY

Having completed this chapter you should now

■ appreciate the importance of recognising and respecting the priorities and values of your colleagues

■ understand the need to relate well to people both as individuals and groups

If you are unsure about any of these areas, go back and re-read the relevant part(s) of the text.

2 UNDERSTANDING THE INDIVIDUAL AT WORK

Personal values are one factor which influence people's attitudes and motivation, but there are other fundamental factors at work also related to basic human needs and satisfactions.

If asked 'Why do people work?' we might suggest two immediate reasons

- for economic survival
- because of social pressure to maintain ourselves and our families

But a moment's thought shows that our motivation in working is much more complex than that of basic survival, important though that is. People constantly make choices about their work - what work to do, who to work for, whether to work hard - for reasons which reflect a whole range of other rewards or satisfactions from their work as well as money or social acceptability.

fig 2.1

In his book 'The Human Side of the Enterprise' **Douglas McGregor** argued that there are two very different approaches to management and motivation and these reflect differences in management beliefs about why people work.

He called the first **Theory X** and saw it as based on three assumptions

- that the average individual has a natural dislike for work and will avoid it if possible
- since most individuals dislike work, they need to be controlled and threatened with punishment if they are to work productively
- most individuals want to avoid responsibility

The second approach to motivation which he called **Theory Y** assumes that

- physical and mental effort at work is natural
- individuals will try to achieve objectives to which they are committed
- most individuals learn to accept and in fact look for responsibility

ACTION POINT 2

Think about the sort of assumptions that are made about people in your company. Which of the two theories seems to you closer to that reality? Note down your view and some brief instances or examples to support it.

The research of psychologists (and probably your own observations) suggest that for most people work is not undertaken solely because of economic necessity or pressure from society (as Theory X would have it), but that

■ the group activity of work can satisfy a range of **human needs** which all individuals share

■ where people are given the opportunity to satisfy those needs through their work they are ready to be motivated to considerable effort to achieve shared goals

In other words it seems to support the Theory Y approach to motivation and management.

Two Theories of Human Needs and Motivation

Anything we do starts from a drive inside us. For instance, if I eat, it is because I am hungry and I have a drive to satisfy that hunger; or even because I fancy a piece of chocolate when I'm not hungry and I am driven to buy and eat some chocolate. In effect, I have needs and **motivation is the drive to satisfy needs.**

Since people tend to behave in ways they believe will bring satisfaction of their needs, if we want to understand what motivates people, we have to consider what those needs are.

Maslow's Hierarchy of Needs

According to the psychologist Abraham Maslow, people's needs are basically similar and can be arranged in a hierarchy, or series of ascending levels, often shown as in figure 2.2.

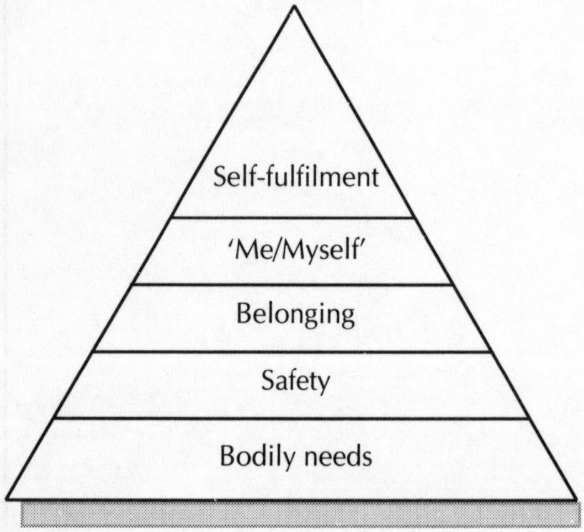

Bodily (or 'Physiological') needs are our most basic and primary needs. Whatever else I need in life, if I am starving to death or deprived of water, or air, or am in mortal physical pain, I will take steps to satisfy those needs at the risk of anything else.

Safety (or 'Security') needs come next, and **only** when bodily needs have been satisfied. If I have eaten, my next concern is to continue to stay alive, both by securing my means of getting the next meal, and by protecting myself from future danger or loss.

Self-fulfilment

'Me/Myself'

Belonging

Safety

Bodily needs

fig 2.2

In the work context, if I earn enough to keep myself and family, I shall want to maintain that situation. I shall want a contract of service, redundancy protection, life and home insurance etc.

Belonging (or 'Social and Affiliation') needs arise according to Maslow **after** I feel secure. People like to feel that they **belong**; so I shall look around to see who is similar, will want my company, ask me to join their group at work or socially. This is a need which can be satisfied through work (but may not be), by my being regarded as 'one of our people' or 'one of the team'.

Me (or 'Ego') needs are to do with being recognised as an individual in your own right, not just being accepted as a member of the group. They are to do with your **contribution to the group**, being **recognised** for special talents or skills or expertise; and they can be particularly satisfied in responsible work on which others rely within group or team activities ('We couldn't do without Pete - he's the only one who can make head or tail of those documents'). This need, perhaps above all others, can be used to motivate staff to achieve work goals.

Self-fulfilment (or 'Self-Actualisation') needs are the final order of needs, those we would pursue if all our other needs were satisfied, so that we were really fulfilling our whole potential.

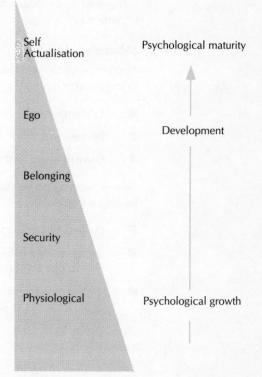

Self Actualisation — Psychological maturity

Ego — Development

Belonging

Security

Physiological — Psychological growth

fig 2.3

Pete may well be the only person who can make head or tail of the documents. But does he think that this is what he was born for? Would Pete be handling the documents still if he won the pools? What in fact would he be doing? Whatever it was it would be **personal and individual** to him since at this highest level of self fulfilment people are all **different**.

As well as classifying needs in this way, Maslow suggests that each lower order need must be satisfied **before** the next higher order need becomes important.

However, your own observations may suggest that this is by no means always correct. In 'Understanding Organisations' Charles Handy argues that man is variable and will have many motives which at any time form a hierarchy, but that **this hierarchy may change** from time to time and from situation to situation, varying for example **in relation to age** or to **stages in the life cycle**, to the **rewards** and **incentives** offered by the organisation and so on. To a person approaching retirement, for example, the security needs related to a company pension may be more important than they would have been twenty years earlier. In the earlier period of working life the need to be recognised for achievement, or doing fulfilling work might have been of much greater importance.

Alderfer's Categories

Another psychologist, Alderfer, classified human needs in a rather simpler way in three categories

- **Existence** needs: survival and reproduction
- **Relatedness** needs: social
- **Growth** needs: personal development

He sees them operating **simultaneously** and not in an invariable sequence, and he also suggests that

- the less a need is satisfied, the more important to us it becomes
- the more a **lower** level need is satisfied the greater the importance of the next higher level need
- the less a higher level need is satisfied the greater becomes the importance of the lower level need

ACTION POINT 3

What implications might these last 3 ideas have for supervisors or managers in relation to motivating individuals?

You may have noted such things as the following

■   if a manager fails to recognise and satisfy a need of a team member (or cannot do so because of organisational constraints) that person will become progressively more dissatisfied with the situation, as the need takes on more importance

■   a manager will always need to be looking for ways to allow their people to develop, as well as simply satisfying their current needs

■   if the job does not allow for much satisfaction of individual growth or recognition needs, things like money, or job security, or bonuses will become more important to the individual and possibly focuses of dissatisfaction

The general importance of the ideas of Maslow and Alderfer for managers is that they focus our attention upon the fact that, as well as satisfying basic money and security needs, work may also be a source of satisfaction (or dissatisfaction) to individuals by meeting (or failing to meet) the social and personal growth needs which almost all human beings share.

ACTION POINT 4

What sort of things might (a) the organisation and (b) the supervisor or manager do to meet the needs of individuals at work? Relate your answers to the following three categories

(i)   Existence or Safety and Bodily needs

(ii)   Social or Relatedness needs

(iii)   Growth or Ego/Self actualisation needs

You might list many things at each level that the organisation and the manager can do. The following are only examples, moving in ascending order through the hierarchy of needs

Organisation

1   Give financial return (wages, salary) enabling bodily needs to be met

2   Give a contract of employment, pension scheme etc so that the employee feels they have stability and 'safety'

3   Provide an organisational 'identity' to which the individual can belong (from such things as a shared company ethos and aims, to details like work clothes reflecting the company identity)

4   Rewards of money, advancement, or company recognition in some form, for achievement or work well done

5   Little directly, though the salary received may enable the individual to do those things which provide self-fulfilment; or where people find self-fulfilment through work achievement, the organisation may be able to provide the scope and responsibility for them to do this

Manager

1   Ensure your people receive the financial returns due to them

2   Ensure they know about company schemes that assist a sense of security; recommend for permanent rather than temporary employment where possible etc

3   Create a team atmosphere amongst your people by consultation, sharing of responsibility and control, linking your section's work to the wider company aims

4   Recognising by individual praise and attention the contribution of each team member; concerning yourself with the person's development

5   Again, little directly, but helping the team member to develop themselves in independence, initiative, and responsibility may considerably contribute indirectly to their self-fulfilment

The common effort and activities involved in work - and particularly in the team context - may give opportunities for people to get satisfaction for their social or relatedness needs. And where opportunities occur for the development and recognition of their skills, abilities and potentials at work, these can be an important way of satisfying their growth, self actualisation and ego needs.

Clearly an individual will be more positively motivated to work the more they are gaining satisfactions from that work. So Maslow and Alderfer direct managerial attention also to the question of matching a person's **needs** with what an organisation can supply in terms of **benefits** (of all kinds) in order to achieve a mutual gain for

- the highest degree of satisfactions for the individual
- the most effective work performance for the organisation

Their work also suggests that given the right circumstances and climate, people will be motivated to commit themselves to groups and objectives which offer them these satisfactions - that McGregor's Theory Y is a more fruitful approach to the management of people than Theory X.

Motivators and Dissatisfiers - Herzberg's Two Factor Theory

The American psychologist Frederick Herzberg looked at work motivation (and its opposite) from a more pragmatic standpoint by asking a sample of employees, 'When you are satisfied at work, what is it that makes you happy?' and 'When you are dissatisfied at work what is it that makes you unhappy?'

Analysing the results, Herzberg found that

- the causes of **satisfaction** at work lie in the contents of **the job itself**
- the causes of **dissatisfaction** lie in the **working environment**

Because the job content factors can create positive satisfaction (and hence motivation) Herzberg called them the **Motivators**. The working environment factors needed to be maintained at a reasonable standard to prevent dissatisfaction and so he called them the **Hygiene** or **Maintenance** factors.

Maintenance or Hygiene Factors

These include such things as

- all aspects of pay - basic, shift and overtime rates, bonuses
- job security
- competent and fair supervision and work support
- all aspects of working conditions
- status and regard given by the organisation to its members
- interpersonal relationships between manager and workteam, and between employees themselves
- company management, organisation and communications

The importance of these factors is their power to cause dissatisfaction if they are not adequate. Even where they are adequate, however, employees will only **be satisfied**, they will not be positively motivated to perform well. Motivation can only occur in Herzberg's view when both maintenance factors and motivators are present in the work situation.

Motivators	Neutral	Hygiene/Maintenance Factors
Satisfaction		Dissatisfaction
Achievement		Working conditions
Recognition		Company policy
The job itself		Bureaucracy
Growth/advancement		Colleague relationships
Responsibility		Supervisor relationships
		Salary

fig 2.4   **Herzberg's Two Factor Theory**

The Motivators

The motivators Herzberg identified appeared to arise from the components of the job content itself. People were motivated if the job gave them opportunities for

■   achievement - personal satisfaction in completing a job, solving problems, seeing successful results

■   recognition - acknowledgement or praise for a job well done

■   growth - opportunities to develop new skills and abilities

■   advancement - opportunities for promotion in the organisation

■   responsibility - degree of control over the work, of work variety, chances to use initiative

It is noticeable that these motivators are all related to the higher level **social** and **personal needs** of people rather than to their basic bodily or security needs. Again they suggest that McGregor's Theory Y is a more fruitful approach to the management of people than Theory X.

ACTION POINT 5

Ken is 22 and a Clerical Officer in the Pensions section of a Social Security office. He has only been there two years but is already accepted by his colleagues as knowledgeable and competent in his work and socially as a pleasant, trustworthy colleague. His supervisor has asked him to train two new entrants on Pensions and told him he can soon expect to be recommended for a Promotions Board. Another senior colleague recently pointed him out to another new entrant as 'One of our best lads - ask him if you have any problems'.

He likes some aspects of his work, such as dealing with people, being able to help pensioners with problems, but he is thinking of the possibility of moving. He finds the regulations don't always permit him to be as helpful as he would like. There is a great deal of pressure of work in the office on everyone (including the supervisor). The pay is not very good in his view, although he can gain some overtime at times when the benefits are uprated and there is extra work to be done. He sometimes finds the work environment depressing and a lot of the work routine.

Which of the factors here would be categorised by Herzberg as 'motivators' and which as 'maintenance factors'?

Ken's situation includes several of Herzberg's motivators. He receives **recognition**, gets some satisfaction from **achievement** (helping the pensioners) and is in line for **advancement**. He has also been given some degree of **responsibility** (the training of others).

The 'maintenance factors' mentioned seem (as Herzberg suggested) to be demotivators in their inadequacy, rather than ones which would positively motivate him if they were present. His working conditions (poor environment, stress, bureaucratic limits to his actions, not very good pay) seem definite demotivators, whilst those apparently adequate factors (job security, competent supervision, communications etc) are not mentioned as positive factors which motivate his work and bring him particular satisfaction.

Critics of Herzberg suggest that a strict distinction between 'motivating' and 'hygiene' factors is often not found in real situations and that a direct link between job satisfaction and productivity does not always exist. In a factory production line, for example, which is unlikely to give much growth or fulfilment opportunity, productivity might be linked very closely with pay rates, bonus schemes and working conditions, and to little else.

In this case the strict distinction between motivators and hygiene factors seems to break down - pay and conditions straddle both categories. But his research does highlight two important messages for those seeking to achieve work goals through other people

- that in most industries **job content** can influence work behaviour as much as factors like pay

- that if people are to be motivated towards high performance rather than minimum standards in achieving work goals, then **the needs for achievement, recognition, responsibility, advancement and growth** - which will vary with individuals according to values, temperament, age, circumstances, and so on - need to be brought into play

Expectations and Motivation

One final theoretical model of why people work – and what is important to them in the work situation - approaches the subject from the **expectations** that individuals have in going to work rather than their needs.

A variety of expectations (of financial, social, personal or psychological satisfactions and rewards) **motivate** us to **effort**, which leads to **performance** giving rise to **reward**, which in turn **motivates** us to greater **effort** and so on. And our continuing motivation to effort will depend upon the expectations of reward being satisfied.

But at any stage in this cycle, obstacles may arise to its effective functioning so that motivation or effort or performance breaks down.

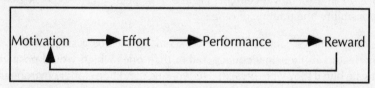

fig 2.5

ACTION POINT 6

Jot down four examples (one for each stage) of breakdowns which might occur in this cycle.

You might have suggested some of the following examples

1   Motivation may not lead to effort where what is expected of the individual is not clearly set out or where the organisation won't let you do something because

   ■   you're too junior, too senior or in the wrong department

   ■   someone else is doing it or you haven't the 'right' training

2   Increased effort may not lead to better performance and reward where

   ■   you don't have the resources or equipment to translate your effort into better performance

   ■   you haven't the training or capability to meet the demands of the task, however hard you try

   ■   feedback hasn't been given to show **how** performance could be improved

3   Performance may not produce the anticipated rewards where

■   an organisation simply doesn't have a system of directly related bonus or reward for reaching targets or attracting new customers

■   your immediate manager or local management does not recognise or value what you have achieved, or doesn't use reward systems that do exist through oversight or ignorance

4   Rewards themselves may not lead to continuing or increased motivation if

■   the individual knows that a particular reward is a 'one-off' incentive or doesn't trust that promised rewards will be honoured

■   what is offered to staff is not something they want

Perhaps the most useful contribution of the expectancy theory cycle is that, like Herzberg, it highlights how **organisational factors** - rules and procedures, resources and equipment, the recognition and rewards system, training provision etc - will interrelate with other factors like needs to affect the motivation and performance of people at work.

CHAPTER SUMMARY

Having completed this chapter you should now

■   understand the factors which motivate individuals at work

■   realise the need to create opportunities for the development and recognition of skills

■   understand the importance of matching a person's needs with what an organisation can supply

If you are uncertain about any of these areas, look back and re-read the relevant parts of the text.

3 MOTIVATION - SOME PRACTICAL CONCLUSIONS

Having looked at a number of influential views about individual needs and expectations - particularly in relation to work - what conclusions, if any, can we draw for management and supervisory practice?

ACTION POINT 7

What does the work of Maslow, Alderfer, Hertzberg, and the expectancy theorists suggest to you that managers and supervisors should be doing in practical terms if they want satisfied and highly motivated individuals in their teams?

Some general observations might include the following

■ human motivation is a complex matter; and management which concentrates only on financial reward and coercive discipline to gain better performance (Theory X) is unlikely to get the best results in pursuing work goals

■ factors affecting commitment and performance range from the most basic (comfort, safety etc), to the most subtle and individual (self image, self fulfilment); some may be important by their absence (Herzberg's hygiene factors), others may be more important by their presence (motivators)

■ the sole judge of what is or is not a motivator or demotivator will be the individual concerned, and not any preconceived theory or practice based on 'the average person'

■ supervisors have little direct influence on some of the more basic factors of motivation (pay and conditions, for example) but are centre stage when it comes to those all important 'higher level' factors such as recognition, achievement, 'belonging', fulfilment, respect and so on

You might also have concluded that almost every aspect of this level of management will have its impact on motivation and performance from how planning, organisation and control operate in the team to the human relations and communications climates which the supervisor will do so much to influence. Some of the practical considerations include the need for the supervisor to

■ get to know their teams as individuals, their values, attitudes, what things personally satisfy/dissatisfy or motivate them at work. (This highlights also the importance of open, honest communication for good team performance)

■ ensure that individuals know clearly what is expected of them; discuss goals and targets and changes which affect the individuals with them rather than presenting them without consultation

■ give people a sense of 'belonging' by building a team climate in which there are no people who are 'in' and others who are 'out'

■ show individuals that their contribution and role is recognised and valued by giving praise or thanks appropriately

■ give well focused and positive feedback about performance routinely, not just at appraisal times, to help motivate and develop them

■ encourage individuals to satisfy their self development needs and improve their skills through training, job rotation etc

■ look for ways to give individuals opportunities for responsibility, autonomy, achievement and recognition by properly supported, progressive delegation

■ consider how job organisation and company rewards systems might be better designed to satisfy and motivate people, and use what influence they can to change these where necessary

■ ensure that staff are capable of the tasks assigned to them

■ ensure staff are properly equipped and equipment is maintained

- keep available resources at the level needed for the individual to perform well

- draw achievements to the attention of reward decision-makers and see that any reward due reaches the staff so that individuals know their effort is not wasted

The practice of delegation, an awareness of job design issues, the proper handling of feedback, good communications, the creation of an open and positive team climate - all these demand particular supervisory knowledge and skills. They also affect not just the motivation of individuals but also the cohesiveness and effectiveness of the team. So we shall look in more detail at these particular issues affecting motivation after we have considered the dynamics of the group and when we look later at the skills of team building.

ACTION POINT 8

A colleague, George Hoyland, has expressed worries to you privately over a drink about his team's performance compared with yours. 'I don't understand how you do it,' he said. 'Your section loading is just the same as mine - same number of staff, same sort of experience and ages - but I always seem to have so much more work on my plate than you. Of course you're lucky with your people,' he went on, 'they seem so energetic and positive. My lot are really unwilling to take on work and don't seem to listen, so I've given up asking them to do the stuff - I do it myself.' He pointed wryly at his bulging briefcase. 'I shall do that lot after dinner,' he said heavily, 'it's the same most nights.'

You arrange to see him again in a couple of days. You knew George had problems. Two people had left his section and there'd been several requests for transfer with complaints that it was no fun to work in his section, he showed little interest in how they were doing because he was always too busy to talk and when he did, he didn't make himself clear as he was in such a rush.

Write down **in outline** the advice you will give him. Concentrate on how he can alter his staff's attitudes to work and towards him as a motivator. List systematically the headings and subheadings under which you would structure your advice.

Compare your thoughts with what follows.

George Hoyland needs to

- spend time getting to know his team and what motivates the individuals in it

- spend time and thought on re-organising himself and the section to take account of this

He needs to understand the importance for most people of opportunities for **achievement, recognition, autonomy and self-development**. He will then see that taking on all the work himself adds to the problems of low expectations, boredom and dissatisfaction in the team. By delegating some of the overload he has accumulated he can get time for essential supervisory tasks and give team members some sense of responsibility and importance in their work.

Having identified people who could be motivated by possibilities of achievement, growth and/or advancement, he should decide in the light of their aptitudes and skills, how to re-allocate tasks and train people to begin to use that motivation and regain their commitment. He should discuss what he proposes with each individual to give them a clear picture of what their responsibilities will be, what control they will exercise, how their tasks should be achieved, any necessary training or resources etc. At the same time he will be signalling his interest in their development and his support, and his expectation of their success. He could also point out to them the advancement of others who have developed themselves in this.

He should begin to look for opportunities to praise and reinforce good performance rather than complain about his staff. If things do need improving, he should give advice supportively, rather than critically, and give a sense to the team that he trusts them to do their best. He should consider the rewards available for good performance in the company, communicate them to his people if necessary, and begin to look for appropriate opportunities to use them, or recommend his team members for them.

CHAPTER SUMMARY

Having completed this chapter you should now

- ■ understand the factors which motivate individuals at work and what these imply for supervisory behaviour and practice

- ■ understand the importance of getting to know your team as individuals

- ■ realise the need to look for opportunities to praise, rather than complain about, your staff

If you are uncertain about any of these areas, look back and re-read the relevant parts of the text.

4 UNDERSTANDING THE GROUP

We have seen how values, needs and expectations will affect the motivation of individuals, but work goals are achieved by groups not simply through individuals; and groups have their own rules and dynamics which exert a powerful influence on the way people behave in them. To be effective any group leader needs to understand

■ why groups form and the stages through which they develop

■ the importance of informal as well as formal groups

■ how groups create their own rules, norms and dynamics - characteristics which make a group more than simply the sum of its parts

■ the importance of group roles and how they evolve

Groups and Why They Form

We have already seen how most individuals like to 'belong', to feel part of a group and so have their worth recognised. These **social** needs for belonging, acceptance and recognition come into play wherever a number of people are required to work together over a length of time. Their contact with each other and being part of common or shared work tasks make them begin to think of themselves as a group, to behave as a group and to form a group identity. They gradually set up, usually without conscious thought to the process

■ group rules of membership and behaviour

■ group standards or norms

■ group roles and relationships

One of the first recognitions of this phenomenon occurred in the Hawthorne Experiments, named after the building at the Western Electrical Company in which they took place. The two main groups of experiments involved observation of two groups of men in a factory workshop, and observation of a group of women working together in a small room at the factory where a succession of changes was made over a period of time in the working terms and environment.

It was noticed (amongst many other findings) that

- the groups either had or developed standards, rules of work behaviour and internal relationships to which the individuals and the group were expected to subscribe; and in return the individuals gained the benefits of group acceptance and recognition

- the men set levels of work in the group which differed from the company's requirement; but they were just as strict with their members who fell below the levels they felt were fair, as with those who exceeded the accepted work levels - and they had ways of 'punishing' anyone who stepped out of line

- the women's work rates improved as a result of **every** individual change that was made to their work conditions, whether favourable or unfavourable. They reacted well to being regarded as special, to being recognised as the experimental group, and to the fact that they were consulted for their opinions by the researchers

The observations not only drew attention to how groups develop an identity and rules and norms of behaviour, but they also showed clearly the powerful effect which groups have on the behaviour and attitudes of individual team members.

Formal and Informal Groups

Groups forming in the work context may be either formal or informal in nature.

Formal Groups (like the staff group of a particular workshop or section or department) are **set up or recognised by the organisation** and they

- exist to perform the ongoing tasks of the organisation or specific individual jobs

- have people appointed by the organisation into certain **official roles** (Chief Technician, Head of Customer Service etc)

- have an officially laid down **structure**, **relationships**, **tasks** and **hierarchy**

Informal Groups within the organisation **form by themselves** to serve social and other needs, and may cut completely across the formal groupings, ignoring the patterns of status and relationships which the formal structures of the organisation have imposed.

An informal group might consist of all those who lunch together in the Griffin for a drink each Friday, or friends from a training course, or users of the company Sports and Social facilities and so on.

The informal group membership can **coincide** with that of a formal group - where a work group all get on together outside work, for example, and see each other socially; but it depends on the situation at a particular time whether they feel themselves a member of one group rather than the other. And where memberships coincide, **the informal leader may well be a different person from the formal leader**.

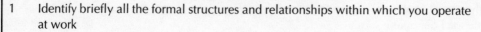

ACTION POINT 9

1   Identify briefly all the formal structures and relationships within which you operate at work

2   Note down an example of one informal and one formal group in your workplace. What influence does belonging to each have on the behaviour of its members?

Compare your observations with the ideas on group influence that follow.

One point you may have noted is that the informal group's influence is often more powerful than that of the formal group; that sometimes, for instance, when management ask its members to do something out of the ordinary, they may look first at the informal leadership to check for the subtle nod of acceptance before agreeing to do it themselves.

The Manager and the Informal Group

It does not often happen in most work teams that the informal and formal groupings wholly coincide, or that they share the same values and attitudes and look to the same leadership. And an informal group withholding its full co-operation or dominating a team can be difficult for a manager, who has no direct control or authority over it by its very nature. Influence can only be exerted on it through their own leadership and team management skills.

How informal groupings within a team are handled will be crucial to success in achieving work goals and the chances of success will be much improved if the manager knows something about **group dynamics** - that is, how groups of both types operate. These include such things as

■　　group boundaries and membership

■　　their norms, rules and sanctions

■　　the developmental processes through which groups go (particularly formal groups)

■　　the roles taken within the group by individual members

Group Boundaries and Membership

Problems or conflicts in a group often concern movement across the group's boundary - the line which defines who is in it and who is outside it. Groups have unwritten **rules** for admission and for expulsion and for subtly defining who is in the group and who is outside it.

ACTION POINT 10

Can you identify

(i)   an admission rule operated by a group you know of?

(ii)   a specific example of the effect of 'in' and 'out' boundaries in operation?

Admission rules will of course vary from group to group.

A person may be admitted to the group if they enter from the bottom, in a low status job; or join via an attachment of some kind with an existing and well regarded group member. (If managers want a new member accepted by an informal group as well as the formal workteam, it is important to remember this in the way they introduce them).

Another route into a formal group is via the top, of course. We cannot reject the new manager formally, though the group may choose informally to withdraw their commitment or to co-operate at only the most minimal level.

Admission may also involve showing yourself willing to be of service to the group and showing an acceptance of the group's working practices and attitudes (through staying an extra few minutes to help out when there is no obligation to do so, for example).

Full admission to the group will show itself when the member 'on trial' is allowed openly to cross the boundaries which indicate membership.

'In' and 'out' boundaries may mean that someone outside the group cannot occupy one particular corner of the bar or a particular table in the canteen; that outsiders do not break in to offer their opinions when a group discussion is taking place (or that their contribution is ignored); or that a person is called Mr Bainbridge by those outside his circle, but Johnny by those within it. A sign of acceptance might be that people begin to use your first name or invite you to use theirs.

Group Norms, Conformity and Sanctions

Once people are admitted to groups they are expected to fall in with the rules or **norms** of proper behaviour, or ways of working, or principles of procedure with which the group agrees to operate.

They are the things we expect of other people and what they in turn expect of us. They will depend on people's jobs and work roles and where they work.

Group Norms

ACTION POINT 11

Try to identify two or three examples of group norms operating within your work team. Think, for example, of how the group treat each other or view other sections, departments or stations.

There are clearly many possibilities.

Norms can concern very small things like nicknames used or 'in group' jargon or small details of work practice. People will show themselves outside the group by saying 'Accounts Department Head Office' where the group refers simply to 'Birmingham'; using group nicknames, or first names, where such familiarity is confined to group members, will provoke irritation and possibly rebuff. Other groups may be treated as inferior or superior, with co-operation, rivalry, indifference and so on.

More importantly norms can determine such things as

■ work levels (as we saw in the results of the Hawthorne experiments)

■ whom we shall like, dislike, talk to, co-operate with, ignore etc

It is also important to realise that **informal group norms** will affect people's behaviour within the formal group and can relate to major or minor matters such as

■ what relationship we will have with the manager

■ how easily we will react to changes in work routine

■ whether we do overtime, and how much

■ whom we will accept, and by what rules

■ how long we spend at lunch and coffee breaks

Norms concerning relationships both within the group and outside must be discovered and acknowledged: trying to get a person to work with someone the group has decided not to co-operate with, is extremely difficult; nor is it easy to change the group's mind on such a matter. The possible consequences of breaking those norms or rules can also be severe for the individual. Awkwardness, disapproval, even rejection by the group can follow.

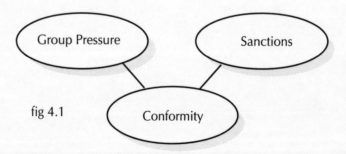

fig 4.1

Conformity

In most cases group rules do not need to be actively enforced - members are inclined to conform to them willingly as the price of meeting the human need to 'belong.'

This tendency to conform is strong. Experiments by many psychologists show that individuals will often agree (or at least go along with) the group even against the evidence of their own eyes. It is even stronger where the group consists of

■ experts in the group's field who are respected by each other

■ people who are important to each other, especially economically

■ people who wish to be liked by each other

■ people who have been together for a long time

The pressure towards conformity is a powerful unifying factor in groups and may be a very positive force where it draws from people a common effort towards well directed goals. But it may also be a powerful force in obstructing team performance if the team or an informal group within the team disagrees with or is uncommitted to the work goals or methods or leadership of a work section.

As well as using the natural tendency of people to conform, groups have ways of disciplining those who don't. These ways are called sanctions.

ACTION POINT 12

Suppose somebody breaks an important norm in a group. Suggest two or three ways in which the group in a work situation might try to make that person change.

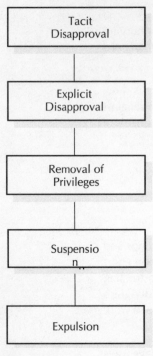

fig 4.2

Sanctions

Sanctions tend to be progressive, depending on the nature and degree of the 'offence', and to go through such stages as

Tacit Disapproval - conveying the group's dislike of what is happening, by a look or gesture or a meaningful word ('Really - Tracy - please!').

Explicit Disapproval - where the rules are 'spelled out' to the offender ('Tracy, surely you realise that we just don't do that sort of thing here').

Removal of Privileges - the limiting of shared information ('Don't tell Tracy Entwistle') or lunching without her, for example.

Suspension ('sending to Coventry') - the group will only talk to her when forced to by the nature of the work, pending reform.

Expulsion from the informal group - and where they coincide, possibly from the formal group too ('OK, that's it Tracy. If you're working here, we are not; as far as we're concerned, you're out').

Finally, there is even **career damage** in the most extreme case: 'We don't know whether you're thinking about Tracy for that new job - but if so, there's something you may need to know about her...'

ACTION POINT 13

What do you see as the implications for managers or supervisors of the existence of group boundaries, norms and sanctions and group pressures to conform?

All these factors - group norms, group boundaries, conformity, pressure and sanctions - will be powerful influences for good or ill in group performance; they will be important cohesive factors in welding group attitudes and behaviour when the group is well led and dynamic, or when it is poorly motivated and uncommitted.

Helping to influence and set the group norms (particularly by example) so that they support good work performance, and being aware of the processes at work will be an important part of leading a team successfully.

The Group Formation and Development Cycle

Behavioural scientists, using and developing terms first suggested by Bruce Tuckman, have argued that any group which eventually forms an effective, cohesive functional unit proceeds through certain identifiable stages.

Stage 1 Infancy ('Forming')

Here group members are finding out who others are, what they can do and how they behave, and trying to establish the **basic criteria and behaviour** it will expect its members to conform to. Individuals will be trying to establish **patterns of relationship, roles and interaction** that they will feel safe and comfortable with. There may well be confusion and anxiety as differing styles and needs become evident; and potential rivalries may show themselves.

Stage 2 Adolescence ('Storming')

Having set a base level of similarities and expectations, the group will move into a stage where **conflicts** develop. Individuals begin to challenge views and attitudes which differ from their own. Regardless of how clear the group structure is, or the task, members may withdraw support from the decisions and approach of the designated leader(s) in bids to establish a **personal identity, influence and importance** within the group, to have control of what they do and some sense of personal direction.

This is a vital, though often difficult stage, since until these **power issues** within the group have been worked out and its **decision-making mechanics** have been established, the group is likely to return repeatedly to these issues without progressing further. By working through the issues openly, the group will gain in its eventual cohesiveness and endurance.

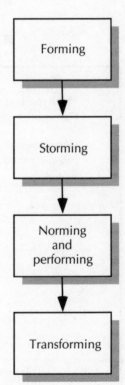

fig 4.3

Stage 3 Adulthood ('Norming and Performing')

At this stage the group begins to pull together. There is now genuine **seeking of agreement**, the development of trust, a give and take approach to finding roles, functional relationships and ways of getting tasks done, despite individual differences. As increasing time and energy are devoted to achieving the team's goals, the ensuing success also has a powerful bonding effect.

Stage 4 Transforming

The final stage of group development occurs when the purpose or goals of a particular group have been achieved. A group is a dynamic thing and does not cease developing, so its next stage is one of change also.

Transforming can take one of two paths

- redefinition of the group - the establishment of a new purpose, new goals or a new structure

- termination or break up of the group

ACTION POINT 14

Think through the process of a group task or project you have recently completed. Can you identify the stages mentioned above as your group went through them?

Write down your views of the process, identifying what sequence and stages your group went through and how these showed themselves in people's behaviour and attitudes.

Variations in the Cycle

Of course the developmental process outlined here will rarely follow this sequence smoothly and continuously. Groups will stick at some stages, move quickly through others, go backwards, then move forward again; Storm and Norm are sometimes reversed. In extreme cases, the storming stage can break the group up, but it is also possible for groups to become effective before conflict arises; where there are personnel or leadership changes, groups may revert to a previous stage and so on.

The important thing for the leader of a newly forming team - particularly in the first two stages - is to be aware of these processes and to understand the group's needs. They can then provide appropriate support and guidance, rather than reacting to the difficulties with anxiety or criticism or even panic.

ACTION POINT 15

What would be the likely problems and needs for team members in the first two stages and how do you think a manager might best help them through these?

How smooth **forming** proves, or how intense and frustrating, will depend broadly upon

- the degree of compatibility of style and needs among members of the group
- the degree of tolerance within the group for the inevitable uncertainty of the first stage

Individuals will look for security, support and guidance. And the leader can encourage people to

■ be prepared to listen to others rather than sticking rigidly to positions and opinions

■ be prepared to exchange knowledge, views and information openly, so that people feel less threatened or uncertain in the situation

Storming can be a frustrating period for everyone and it is important that the manager does not react negatively to the criticisms, problems and conflicts it produces. A number of areas may produce tensions. Individuals may see their jobs within the group differently and have very different views of priorities and procedures at first. Some people may seek to establish dominant positions in the group and this may be resented by others. Adjustments have to be made to the first agreements. People may find they cannot work the way they agreed earlier, or lose each other's confidence, or discover difficulties in the characters of others, or find that the tasks are not sensibly allocated. These difficulties come to a head, and may be rancorously discussed. People will naturally get on with some people in the group better than with others, or find it difficult to establish a good working relationship with people who are different from them in age, outlook or temperament. Such things will all require working through with a conscious effort from all the group.

Supportive supervision is a critical factor here in

■ encouraging the open expression of differences of viewpoint and constructive criticisms rather than attempting to suppress them as 'problems'

■ fostering respect for the position of others and discouraging personal or destructive criticism

■ taking responsibility for initiatives and actions and keeping attention focused on the team's work goals whatever roles and relationships are being established

Group Roles

Another important feature of group dynamics is the way that individuals take on particular **roles** within the group. Individuals want to feel they make a unique contribution to the group and are recognised for that. There may be an ideas person, a peace-maker, a joker, a procedures expert and so on.

ACTION POINT 16

Think for a few minutes about people in a group at work. Write down some of the group roles different individuals adopt. To what aspects of the team's work does each role primarily contribute?

You may have found that most of the roles you thought of could be classified into two kinds of role - **task roles** and **social or group maintenance roles**.

Task roles would cover the individual who is

- good at co-ordinating others in the group, helping them discuss and pool ideas

- good at explaining jobs to others or helping out in difficulties

- reliable in finding out or chasing up others to get the necessary information

- good at problem solving, or coming up with new or different ways of doing things

Social or group maintenance roles relate to how people get on in the group and would involve the person who

- gives support to others in the group, with whom problems can be discussed

- organises group events or social activities

- tries to clear up misunderstandings or upsets in the group

Belbin's Group Roles

A group theorist called **Belbin** has suggested that a well-constructed team would contain various types with particular characteristics which together would advance the team process effectively.

Of course, in practice a work group may be small in number and may not have individuals with the particular characteristics called for in each role, so that in them some members may contribute to or fill more than one of these roles. But his list does indicate a range of characteristics needed for the successful achievement of complex work tasks and most teams, big or small, will find they may have problems where

■ there are role gaps in the team

■ one person is taking on too many roles

■ a person is taking the wrong role

Belbin's ideal team would have

A Chairperson - a disciplined thinker who would organise and co-ordinate the team, maintaining a balance of effort. The central fulcrum of the group, keeping it 'on course.'

A Shaper - an outgoing, creative character who gives dynamism and drive to the group, providing motivation and energy, and some leadership in the more enterprising tasks.

A Plant - often a more withdrawn, thoughtful person, providing ideas for progress by contemplating problems, quietly and privately. Not keen on the limelight, this person may need drawing out at times.

A Monitor Evaluator - a person who carefully evaluates ideas and arguments to check their validity, spots problems in creative approaches, and checks on the accuracy and effectiveness of suggestions and solutions.

A Resource Investigator - the fixer who sets up information and social networks to information and resources, and has many contacts. Likely to be relaxed and outgoing.

A Company Worker - the vital efficient team member who gets on with the job, knows the procedures and has a realistic approach, sees that records are properly kept, keeps timetables and progress charts up-to-date - and does not particularly want a more 'responsible' or 'important' role.

A Team Worker - one who tries to maintain the group as a team, working unobtrusively to see that there is harmony, resolving conflicts, listening to problems, smoothing relationships, pushing others forward.

A Finisher - who drives and persuades and nags the group to meet deadlines and comply with controls. Sometimes anxious; gives the group a sense of urgency when it needs it.

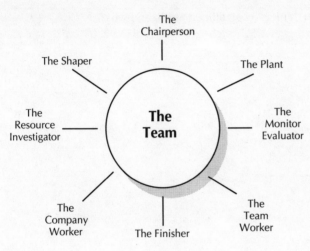

fig 4.4

The significance of these role types is their complementary, balancing nature. Together they will help provide the mix of task and relationship care which can ensure that motivation, team spirit and task concern are all maintained so that work goals are effectively pursued. And it is important for managers to recognise that where there are significant gaps which are not recognised or go unfilled, there will be adverse effects on performance.

ACTION POINT 17

Take a look at your own team, then answer the following questions.

1   Which of the roles in Belbin's model can you identify in your team?

2   Are there any other roles or types in your team not mentioned by Belbin?

3   Which role(s) do you find yourself playing most often?

4   Which role do you think is most difficult to fill, and why?

The **evolution of satisfactory group roles** is a vital part of the development of a cohesive team. Where group roles do not fit the strengths, needs and aspirations of individuals in the team there will be disharmony and tensions. Individuals will be unhappy in roles which do not suit or satisfy them; and the team will be resentful if individuals decline to contribute in the way the team wants them to.

Group Theory - Some Conclusions

ACTION POINT 18

What seem to you the most significant factors that group theory draws attention to for the manager or supervisor and what practical implications do you see them as having for the manager? Make a brief list of what you see as the important points arising from it.

You may well have concluded that group theory in general reinforces the idea that belonging to and being accepted as a valued member by a successful group satisfies important needs for individuals. You may also have suggested that if the group is to develop into a team and reach work goals effectively the manager will need to

■ be aware of and try to influence positively the formal group rules and norms so that a shared concern for high work standards and a high regard for team achievement are central to these

■ create an open, supportive climate in which the establishment of team roles and relationships and influence can be worked through positively, making the best use of everybody's talents and keeping work goals centrally in mind

■ be aware of any informal groupings within the team, and their values and norms, and try to influence and manage them positively to ensure that no 'in' and 'out' groups take root

■ be sensitive to the preferred and most productive group roles of team members (as well as the role needs of the team), try to get the best balance and encourage individuals if need be to 'try out' missing roles

■ look out for, and deal with, situations where group pressures, norms or sanctions, or inappropriate roles may be having a negative effect on individuals and on team performance

■ involve the group in planning and decision making wherever possible to encourage a team outlook and identity

■ look for situations in which more autonomy and responsibility may be given to the group so as to increase team identity, cohesion and achievement

There are many other items of detail you might have mentioned but we could sum up the implications in a single phrase as the need for leadership, awareness and positive team building if a group is to become a team and achieve goals effectively. And these are the areas we shall now look at.

CHAPTER SUMMARY

Having completed this chapter, you should now

■ understand the dynamics of groups and their processes and what these imply for supervisors' behaviour and practice

■ realise the need to influence and set group norms so they support good work performance

■ understand the importance of listening to others rather than sticking rigidly to positions and opinions

If you are uncertain about any of these areas, look back and re-read the relevant parts of the text.

5 LEADERSHIP THEORY AND PRACTICE

Leadership is one of the most critical factors for success in pursuing any objectives through a group. But to identify what good leadership consists of is not the simple matter it may first appear. A group may be successful or unsuccessful under a single, strong leader of authority depending on the people, the type of task and the circumstances; one group where there appears to be only a shared informal leadership may be very successful, whilst another similar group may be an unproductive shambles. What is certain is that without effective leadership (whether formal or informal, single or shared) both individuals and group are likely to feel directionless, dissatisfied and demotivated.

Leadership Theory

ACTION POINT 19

Write down briefly your own ideas of what good leadership is.

Theories of leadership have developed greatly in recent times. At one time much emphasis was given to trying to identify the qualities of 'born leaders'. That accent on the innate qualities of the individual leader is found in **Trait Theory** which asked questions such as, Who were the great leaders? What innate qualities made them great leaders? What traits or characteristics of their behaviour can be used as role models for leadership in industry and commerce?

Although this approach did highlight certain qualities that good leaders demonstrate, like initiative or the ability to see specific situations in a broad perspective and not lose sight of overall aims (sometimes called the 'Helicopter Trait'), it does **not** provide any list of characteristics which everyone would agree upon as marking out a good leader, nor does it say how these desired personality traits and characteristics may be acquired!

Whilst we have to live with traits, **behaviour** can be changed and new **skills** developed, and nowadays leadership is seen as much more about how individuals can use to best effect the qualities they have in organising, influencing and gaining the commitment of a team for their work objectives. It is also about drawing the best from others and responding to change, drawing people to new agendas, allowing them responsibility and autonomy, creating teams and meeting the needs which they have to do their work well.

Style Theory

Style Theory assumes that certain styles of leadership, certain types of **behaviour**, will tend to induce a team to work harder or more effectively than other styles. The styles compared usually fall within a continuum which reflects the degree of **supervisory direction** and the degree of **team participation** in decision making and control of the team's activities. The names generally given to the styles are

- authoritarian
- paternalistic
- laissez faire
- democratic

An extreme **authoritarian style** focuses power totally on the leader who has authority for making all decisions and controls rewards and 'punishment'. The **paternalistic** style shows a greater concern for 'selling' decisions to the group members rather than for telling and imposing, but is still based on decisions being largely made by the leader 'for the benefit' of the team. The **laissez faire** style allows group members to 'do their own thing' and develop their own relationships and influence structures, the leader's status being little different from that of the rest of the group. In the **democratic style** the individual group members are consciously involved in the decision making and control of group activities, and authority and power are shared with the group.

Style theory assumes that people tend to respond more productively under democratic than under authoritarian conditions.

ACTION POINT 20

Think back to the Theory of Human Needs we looked at earlier. Why might it lead us to expect team members to work more productively under democratic than under authoritarian leadership?

We can relate this back to the notion that increased participation in decision-making and responsibility is likely to better satisfy the 'internal' needs or self actualisation needs of the individuals in the team, so that their involvement and commitment will be greatly increased.

The expectation that where people are given opportunity to satisfy more of their social and self fulfilment needs in the work situation they will work with more involvement and effectiveness is supported by available research. In the 1930s a psychologist called **Lewin,** researching different leadership styles in a boys' club, found that the group was most productive under an autocratic leadership style, but that the leader **had** to be there for this to occur and continue. If the authoritarian leader was not continuously present, productive effort fell away sharply. A democratic leadership style was by far the most popular and the most consistent in productivity and quality. A laissez faire style rated poorly in all aspects with little cohesion and direction.

The effect of leadership style upon the degree of initiative, judgment and personal responsibility which team members could use - and hence upon their motivation and commitment - was summed up by Tannebaum and Schmidt showing how there will be a varying balance between the degree of authority used by the manager and the degree of discretion used by the team members according to the style of management adopted. They went on to argue that leaders should not adopt any one leadership style but should change their behaviour according to circumstances and adapt it to the people being led and to the situation.

Realistically most supervisory managment jobs, unless of an extremely straightforward operational nature, will involve a number of different tasks and will require a manager to adopt different leadership styles with the same group of people.

Where particular tasks or core duties are particularly well defined and must be completed to prescribed standards, in a certain order, in a short time a directive management style may be in order. There is less time available for group decisions and once duties have been defined and allocated, further discussion may be unnecessary to their efficient completion. Similarly where personnel are lacking in experience or knowledge, it may be necessary at times to be directive.

But with other relatively open-ended tasks, a competent and balanced workteam, and available time, there may be opportunity for an open, consultative, democratic management style. A directive style would be likely to cause resentment where it is not necessary and where team members have expertise and experience.

Contingency and Situational Leadership Theory

Developments of style theory such as **Contingency Theory** and **Situational Leadership** took the same position and focused upon what factors have to be considered in choosing a leadership style in particular circumstances.

They lay emphasis upon variable factors which are discussed below.

The Task

As tasks are often fixed and not susceptible to change, they may influence or even dictate a particular leadership style at times by

- **the nature of the task itself** - Is it **making** decisions, or carrying them out? Is it routine, or does it involve new problems?

- **the time scale** - Is time available for consultative leadership?

- **the complexity of the task** - The more complicated and difficult, the more a leader may need to manage this complexity. Depending on team maturity, the manager might act directively, or simply initiate structures and provide support

- **the risk factor** - In certain operational and financial contexts, the room for error may be very slim (eg. safety considerations or where large amounts of money are involved) and so management style may need to be strongly directive for everyone's sake

The Group

The leader needs to consider what Situational Leadership refers to as the 'maturity level' of the group, their

■ education, training and experience relative to the task in hand

■ willingness and ability to take responsibility

■ capacity to set high attainable goals and pursue them together

The Context

Like the task, the organisational context - the structure, technology, control systems and culture - will affect the style in which managers operate. Rules and procedures or particular operational methods may not allow you to delegate and develop your team's autonomy in the way you think would be most effective. And though you may be able to make suggestions, or argue for structural or technological and system changes, you will almost certainly have to accept and work within such constraints in the shorter term.

Preferred Style

Weighing up situations and applying an appropriate leadership style is easily said, but it is a matter of simple observation to realise that a manager's or supervisor's own personality, experience and values will naturally predispose them towards a **preferred style** of their own - paternalistic, democratic, or directive as maybe. And they are unlikely to be comfortable (or convincing) in a style totally foreign to their own nature. What leaders **can** do is to give conscious thought to this; and to recognise that some situations will be better dealt with if they try to be more directive, or less directive, or more democratic etc than they would normally be by nature.

A manager who likes to involve and consult the work team, can recognise that with inexperienced staff on well-defined, urgent tasks, their own natural inclination may need to be overcome and they need to adopt a 'directive' style. Or a naturally forceful manager who enjoys showing others how to do things and 'getting stuck in' may recognise the need to curb that tendency if team members are to be given opportunities to develop.

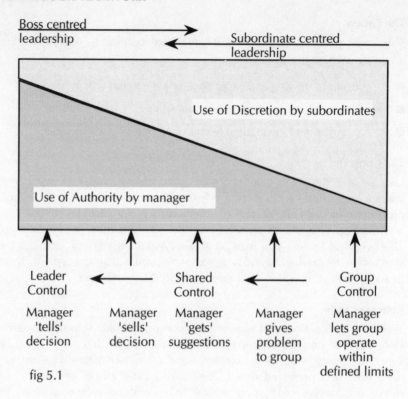

fig 5.1

ACTION POINT 21

Consider the following situations

1   You are manager of an electrical servicing department in an expanding company. Your current premises are too small and you are about to move into new, custom-built offices. Unfortunately, the move falls at your busiest time of year and you have a slight staff shortage.

You have a regular team of 6: 4 general servicing technicians, 1 senior servicing engineer and 1 floater (who deals with queries, emergencies and other problems). However, three of the technicians are relatively new and on the first day of the move you find the experienced floater will be off sick for a week. Though the two remaining members of your team are experienced and trustworthy, they are not so inclined to take a lead as the floater would have done.

As well as transportation, the move means detailed customer records and other files have to be rationalised, logged, repackaged and stored. Certain key information has to be entered on computer for the first time, ready for the new operation. All this has to take place over ten days, with minimum disruption to customer service.

There are set procedures from head office (modified by yourself) for effecting the operation, and normally you would happily leave the team to get on with most of it after a participative group discussion about tackling it. However, as your team is now, you feel much less confident. But decisions about who does what, how and by when - and what control and monitoring will take place - need to be arrived at quickly with your team.

2   You are a team leader in the marketing department of an electrical goods manufacturing firm. You are relatively new to this firm and industry but have 5 years research and marketing experience and have quickly built up a reputation as a good delegator and co-ordinator with energy and vision. As a result, you have been asked to head up the development of plans for launching a new top-of-the-range product.

The design specifications are in the advanced stages, a production plan is near completion and you will have to liaise closely with the company's advertising agency and internal departments. But you have access to the skills of your own and other departmental teams from whom you can draw a 'task force' of personnel as well as any information or co-operative action you require.

You, and the team you select, have been asked to come up with a detailed marketing plan and an analysis of implications for other departments inside one month.

Bearing in mind the nature of the tasks involved, do you think your managerial style or approach would differ in the two situations? Write down in broad terms how you would approach each and, if your supervisory managerial approach would be different, explain why.

The two situations demand very different handling.

In Situation 2 there is a variety of talent available and time to get small groups together to work on all aspects of the task. There is the opportunity for an open, supportive and democratic style to be used. A directive style would be likely to cause resentment.

In Situation 1 it would not be feasible to involve everyone in decisions about how to do the task. It is clearly designed and must be completed to prescribed standards done in a certain order in a short time. Directive leadership is required, using your own experience and the experienced team member to check on the work of the less experienced.

A Practical Approach to Leadership

A different and very practical approach known as **action-centred leadership** has been advocated in recent years by John Adair, starting from the basic assumptions that in any group there are needs which must be met if individuals and group are to function well and get satisfaction from their work

The better a leader understands these and takes **observable actions** to satisfy them, the better the leader. The three sets of needs he identified are

■ **Task Needs** - A group has a need to get its tasks done well

■ **Team Needs** - A group has the need to maintain cohesion, spirit, teamwork and morale

■ **Individual Needs** - Each member of the group has individual needs which membership of the group helps to satisfy

Adair's model is always shown as a set of overlapping circles since

■ many actions can satisfy more than one type of need

■ it indicates how interrelated these needs and activities are and how important it is for leaders to do things which will satisfy all three sets of needs

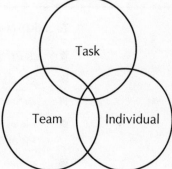

fig 5.2

Task Needs

A task or series of tasks to do together is what gives that identity of purpose which characterises a team. And because of **the need to achieve** and **be recognised** for achievement, the response of any normal group is to wish to do the task well rather than badly. For these reasons, Adair says

Groups look to the leader to see that they do well

They expect the leader to **do things** - to see to it that the tasks get done. And if the leader does not do these things, not only will task completion suffer, but team dissatisfaction and demotivation will follow.

ACTION POINT 22

What can the leader do? List the observable actions you think a leader can take to satisfy task needs.

To satisfy task needs a leader must

- grasp their own brief and understand its details

- get all the necessary information from superiors and other sources

- define, discuss, agree and write down objectives and targets

- clearly divide up tasks; define them, allocate them according to skills, training, inclinations

- make a plan of action and be seen to stick to it

- obtain, and at least be seen to fight for, all necessary resources to enable staff to perform well

- invite and listen to suggestions from qualified or experienced staff and others

- set up systems and time scales of control and operate them scrupulously; maintain task timing

- monitor internal and external influences and communications which may affect the progress of the task; and communicate them to others as necessary

It is evident that none of these require any **personal** characteristics except having personally identified oneself as leader. They can be **done** by introverts or extroverts, the humorous or the solemn, the faster or the slower thinker, provided that they have simply determined to do them.

Team Needs

Teams also have needs. If asked to choose between being a member of

■ a low morale group, with constant conflict, no trust, no sense of achievement and no discipline

■ a high morale group with agreed rules of procedure and sound relationships, high personal standards and group achievement

any individual would choose the second. Teams need cohesion, high morale and achievement and they look to the leader to take the actions necessary which will help them to feel good about themselves as a group.

ACTION POINT 23

What can the leader do? List the observable actions you think a leader can take to satisfy team needs.

To satisfy team needs a leader must

- tell the group its objectives, targets and tasks clearly - and the reasons for them

- obtain group agreement to those overall tasks and targets

- monitor and summarise progress regularly, giving constructive feedback about its performance and praising its achievements

- maintain harmony; face up to and resolve conflict positively

- defend, and be seen to defend, the group against outside attack

- foster a constructive, open climate in which the team can express ideas and feelings without fear and where there is mutual trust and a sense of common purpose

Again these are things that managers can **do** to satisfy needs, to lead and motivate their team, regardless of their own particular character and personality.

Individual Needs

Earlier we saw how people bring to their work their **individual needs** for survival and security, social relationships and recognition, growth and self-fulfilment. As well as looking for team satisfactions, they will look to their managers to help them to satisfy their individual needs at work.

ACTION POINT 24

What can the leader do? List the observable actions you think a leader can take to satisfy individual needs.

To satisfy individual needs a leader must

- check on the special skills and knowledge of individuals in the group

- discover the personal likes and dislikes of each for various aspects of the group's work

- give individuals opportunities for responsibility, achievement and recognition in their tasks

- clearly communicate what each task involves to the jobholder

- consult, listen, give advice, support and reassurance where appropriate

- keep each person in touch with their personal standards and progress and achievements

- defend individuals against attack of any sort from outside the group, including attack by organisational superiors

- acknowledge special achievements and make them known to significant other people

- see to it that where there are organisational rewards available and deserved, they are awarded

- encourage individuals to develop by correcting poor practice, owning their own problems, training for new skills, and taking on new tasks

- acknowledge each individual's role in the group, enhancing their feelings of belonging and morale

Leading by Example, Establishing Trust

One other aspect of leadership in relation to team building is worth considering before we look in more detail at some of the skills involved.

Whether leadership is action centred or style centred or pragmatic and ad hoc, a leader will always be, willingly or not, **a model** for their team. And poor leadership will have as much an influence upon team members as good leadership.

If a leader is aiming to build a group where individuals

- have high personal and group work standards

- work as a team and achieve their goals

- confront issues as they arise and are open and honest in their communications and relationships

- use judgement and initiative and take responsibility for their actions then they need to model that behaviour themselves in their work and work relationships. Amongst other things they will be seen to

■ be true to personal beliefs and be regarded as having integrity by others

■ face facts and problems honestly

■ be open, not manipulative in their dealings

■ use delegation to aid achievement and development, not as a way of reducing their own workload

■ give trust and loyalty to their team and support it strongly both inside and outside the group

■ be accessible and receptive to others and respect their needs

■ be reliable in establishing clear goals and standards and effective working practices

In doing so they will also create that basic prerequisite of effective team building - a sense of **trust** between leader and team. Trust is established where there is

■ consistency

■ predictability

■ reliability

It is not present where people do not say what they mean, do not mean what they say, talk about others behind their backs, betray confidences, give information or advice which is unreliable, untimely or self-interested, do not meet commitments or warn of problems and do not openly face up to issues which need to be worked through to a clear resolution.

CHAPTER SUMMARY

Having completed this chapter you should now

■ understand how leadership and actions relate to performance

■ be ready to put into practice appropriate behaviours to satisfy team, task and individual needs

■ understand the need to monitor and summarise progress regularly and resolve any conflict positively

■ realise the importance of being accessible and receptive to others

6 BUILDING THE TEAM

ACTION POINT 25

Bearing in mind what we have so far discussed, what would you expect to characterise the climate and approach in a team as opposed to a group?

You may have noted such things as

- people working purposefully together for clearly shared goals in an atmosphere of mutual trust and confidence and concern for performance

- an acceptance of differences and of the contributions and roles of each individual

- the resolution of differences positively without personal animosities

- the ready sharing of knowledge, information, skills and abilities, rather than their use as personal power bases

■ individuals not feeling threatened by problems in their work but able to state them openly and use the team as a resource and support

■ the sharing and delegation of responsibility with people working independently but co-operatively

■ individuals not feeling threatened by others' suggestions as to how performance in their work area might be improved

■ individuals not afraid to take initiatives and actions as needed, not being constrained by fear of disapproval

As we noted earlier in the book, there are actions leaders can take and skills they can develop and apply to satisfy team needs and to positively set about the building of teams. We shall look at these in the chapters which follow.

Developing Team Awareness

We have seen how groups affect the behaviour, relationships and performance of individuals through their norms and rules, and through the roles which evolve in a team. Managing a team demands an awareness not only of these things, but also of the processes - particularly group communication and decision making processes - which will need to be managed or influenced if both individual contributions and a co-operative team spirit are to be maximised.

Considered actions and interventions by a supervisor or manager may benefit the team process greatly if they are aware of such factors as

■ **the degree of acceptance or inclusion** of individuals in the group which in many cases may be indicated by the amount of **verbal participation** by individuals

Are there any subgroups whose members consistently agree and support each other, and oppose others? Are some people 'outside' the group? How are they treated? Do some move in and out as if not fully committed? Under what conditions?

Why are some high and some low participators? What does a member's silence indicate? How do the group respond to their silence? Who talks to whom? Who keeps the ball rolling?

■ **the degree of influence** people have in the team - which may not always be reflected in their participation. Some people may speak little, yet have the attention of all. Others may talk a lot but not be listened to. Which members are high in influence and which low? Who shifts through influence? What kind of influence - negative or positive - do people wield? How do others react to their influencing style? What would be the likely effects where the group was given greater autonomy and responsibility? Are there leadership rivalries in the group? What effect do they have on other members?

- **the way group decisions are arrived at** - do individuals or subgroups make decisions and carry them out without consulting group members? What effect does this have? Do some individuals or groups try to push decisions through over other members' objections? Or is there always an attempt to get consensus decisions? What seems to be the effect of the chosen approach?

Does anyone make contributions which receive no response or recognition? What is the effect on them? Does the group drift from topic to topic? Who topic-jumps? Why does this happen?

- **the need for task and maintenance functions to be looked after** in a successful team; are there people who can, and do, look after task functions? - making suggestions as to how to proceed or tackle a problem; flagging topics for discussion; summarising what has been covered or decided; keeping the group on course by reminding them of target dates and deadlines; seeking or giving facts, ideas, opinions, feedback, or searching for alternatives

Are there others who contribute to maintaining group morale and relationships and creating a team atmosphere? - by drawing all team members into discussions (gate openers); helping others to clarify issues and ideas; giving praise and showing enthusiasm for others' suggestions when in agreement; rejecting others' ideas in a supportive rather than destructive way; drawing people back to course tactfully rather than offensively (gate closers); listening to problems and being sensitive to feelings; trying to maintain a friendly, congenial co-operative atmosphere, to depersonalise situations of conflict or bad feeling and find solutions without 'winners' and 'losers'

fig 6.1

ACTION POINT 26

How do you think developing such team awareness may help the manager or supervisor in team building?

Awareness of these factors will tell the manager a great deal about the dynamics and relationships of the team and its mood, morale and motivation in any situation. It will provide the grounding from which to manage and influence what is happening, to encourage, to intervene, to change situations, to anticipate and defuse problems, to bring out hidden feelings or blocked contributions and so on.

Gaining the support and commitment of those of high influence or countering negative influences; spotting conflicts or rivalries and dealing with them positively; helping personally with task and maintenance functions in any situation where they seem to be lacking, but encouraging team members to take on such roles - these are only a few of the ways in which the manager will need to act to foster team unity and cohesion; but effective action will depend very much on an initial awareness of the processes at work.

Creating the Right Climate

Individuals in teams will have a variety of backgrounds, values and expectations. To work effectively together they must be able to give of themselves and to accept such differences without animosity or anxiety. Managers therefore need to recognise the feelings generated between members in work interactions or group discussions and to encourage openness. Such feelings may not always be talked about, but can be guessed from tone of voice, facial expressions and other non-verbal clues.

ACTION POINT 27

Consider a group discussion you have been involved in lately.

1   Jot down any unexpressed feelings you observed in group members (anger, disagreement, defensiveness etc). What signs gave those feelings away?

2   Did you see any attempts by group members to block the expression of feelings, particularly negative feelings? How is this done?

3   What do you think managers can do to encourage openness and a constructive climate in the team?

A constructive climate of mutual support and co-operative effort is helped by

- encouraging people to see the group as a resource for ideas, 'know how', help and support

- encouraging people to involve themselves with constructive suggestions in any area of the team's work

- encouraging people to use initiative and take action in the interests of the team and its goals where they judge it is needed

- making sure that formal meetings and discussions of the group are handled efficiently, but that all people who want to contribute are heard and accorded respect

- encouraging people to work through problems or disagreements openly and constructively and not suppressing or blocking them

Climate and Communications

Two of the most basic processes in getting work done and achieving goals are

- the sharing of needed information, ideas and even problems among the group

- the ongoing process of monitoring and giving feedback about group tasks and performance

And the willingness with which information is shared and the readiness of people both to give and to accept evaluative feedback about their work are two of the most important pointers to a team's maturity and strength.

There is of course a need for communications of all kinds about work tasks to be unambiguous and clearly intelligible, and even in the most straightforward circumstances the manager always needs to probe for understanding and to check that messages have been heard and 'taken on board'; but where people find themselves with problems, or differing in their opinions, or feeling critical of another's performance, or in any circumstances where their feelings or self esteem are involved, it is particularly easy for communication to become negative or distorted or even blocked altogether.

ACTION POINT 28

Note down some specific circumstances where open communication between group members can be inhibited - either general examples or instances from your own experience - and comment on the results.

The most important contributions the manager can make towards creating an open communications climate in the team are

■ by being open and honest in their own communications, but focusing any suggestions for improvement on the job being done and never being personally critical

■ by themselves sharing information, ideas, concerns and problems with team members

■ by listening and respecting the integrity of other views in the team

■ by receiving 'bad news' about a situation, or differing views, or critical feedback about their own decisions and actions without reacting negatively or personally

This last point is particularly important. If a manager takes no action when told of impending problems, or becomes defensive or hostile to people in the face of disagreements, their team members will react similarly themselves and in addition are likely to stop communicating information which produces the hostile or negative reactions.

Handling Conflict

Creating this kind of team climate involves handling - and even at times encouraging - the open expression of critical judgements, differing views and conflicting attitudes.

We saw earlier in this book how **norms** may develop in a group that powerfully influence the behaviour of its members, even unconsciously. Often these norms will facilitate group progress, but some may hinder it

■   do the norms mean that group members are always nice or polite to each other? Are only positive feelings expressed? Do members agree with each other too readily? What happens when members disagree? It is possible where these group norms prevail that all critical comment is inhibited, performance is not properly reviewed, and issues which need to be looked at squarely and resolved are not worked through

■   is there an implicit contract 'not to rock the boat'? Team members may consider that critical analysis might undermine morale by exposing weaknesses

Another reason for an unwillingness to be open may be a sense of **inadequate skills**. Although team members may appreciate the benefit of having an intensive review, they may lack the skills of analysis and personal confrontation required.

However, if a team is to be successful, its members must be able to state their views about each other and air differences without fear of ridicule or retaliation. Effective teams don't avoid delicate or unpleasant issues but confront them, honestly.

Handling Conflict Constructively

Conflict can be **destructive** or **constructive**. It depends on a number of factors and how it is handled.

Positive conflict, properly managed and constructively employed, leads to greater understanding and openness, reduced tension, better relationships and more trust within a team.

However, any conflict will become destructive if it

■   becomes personal

■   drags on too long

■   becomes too intense

■   becomes too frequent

and **negative conflict** breeds mistrust and hostility.

The positive handling of conflict means

■ looking for **solutions** - not for somewhere or someone to blame

■ avoiding turning confrontations or conflicts into **win/lose** situations

---

ACTION POINT 29

In a situation where two team members seem to find it very difficult to work together, you decide to move one of them onto other tasks, looked on informally as lower grade work.

Jot down below your thoughts on how each person might feel in the situation and how it might affect their work.

This is a classic **win/lose** situation.

The **winner** feels justified and successful in their personal battle, but pride in 'seeing off' the other person is unlikely to enhance their team behaviour in future or the confidence of their colleagues in them.

The **loser**'s self confidence will have taken a bad knock. Future co-operation is unlikely. Since self esteem has been affected, that team member may withdraw or blame others, and become embittered about colleagues and what happens at work.

Clearly a win/lose situation will usually have unfavourable effects on both individuals and the team as a whole.

What other ways are there of dealing with a conflict situation? Let's look at another example.

ACTION POINT 30

Suppose you are a manager aware that two members on your team have been having differences which ended today in a blazing row, but you don't know what it was about.

Jot down your thoughts on the possible outcomes of these courses of action

1   You decide to ignore it.

2   You take one of the individuals aside and persuade that person to back down now, but promise that next time you'll definitely sort the situation out for them.

3   You decide you will simply work out and present to them a swift, clear solution to the problem without further arguments or a post mortem on what happened, and you'll put up with any aggrieved feelings that follow from either or both of them.

You may take the first course of action if you feel that the problem is short term and may 'go away'. But if the row is the visible result of 'simmering' problems, it is likely that things will get far worse if they are ignored.

If you decide to suppress the conflict (the second course of action) you may provide an immediate solution but you haven't really resolved the issues. Smoothing things over in this way may seem the necessary immediate course of action if under pressure, but the underlying conflict will need to be dealt with.

The third approach may also bring a short term solution, but since neither individual had any say in it they are unlikely to feel much commitment to it. You are likely to have created another win/lose situation where only you are seen as the winner.

Another approach to confrontation is to **seek compromise** - to work through the situation, taking everybody's viewpoint into account as far as possible, and try to work out an acceptable solution.

There are clearly no outright winners or losers in this approach, but it is likely to be a very time consuming process and to involve other issues besides the immediate conflict. Since compromise means that nobody gets exactly what they want, commitment to the solution might again be low.

Neither party will come out of it feeling that they are 'losers'.

However, if people are encouraged to **air their differences openly and fully in a purposeful way** - to clear the air, to fully explain their position and feelings to the other person, to look for a solution - the time may be well spent, with the atmosphere and relationships likely to be better and more constructive afterwards.

There are also advantages in sitting down and working together on a **different** problem

- people are more likely to channel their energies positively rather than into their dispute with each other

- an opportunity is given for 'peace signals' to be passed between people away from the disputed area

- they have a common interest in finding a solution and have to work together

- they may get to know each other better and each other's point of view

- the original source of conflict may become relatively unimportant

Again such collaborative sessions take time to run and they do depend to some degree on an underlying wish for differences to be resolved.

Pre-empting Harmful Conflict

Of course the managerial aim must be to harness the energy created within a group whilst working through the conflicts that arise **before** they become harmful. But it is not easy to strike the balance between giving people freedom to innovate and use their talents, and preventing that energy spilling over and causing conflicts between the individuals who make up a team.

Managers are more likely to succeed in this if they constantly

- check the balance of roles in the team and watch for anyone who is 'miscast'

- involve the team as much as possible in decisions that affect them

- ensure that each person knows what is expected of them and has clear goals

- avoid creating win/lose situations and prevent resentments building up

Using Delegation to Motivate and Develop

As well as creating a team climate and dealing with the dynamics of a group situation, team building is about **sharing responsibility** and **opportunities for achievement and development**. In this way, not only will individuals in the team be better motivated from a personal point of view, as we have seen, but the spreading of responsibility will mean that

- the whole work enterprise becomes much more team oriented

- it brings into play those powerful needs for approval and recognition which motivate people to contribute well to the team endeavour

Delegation is a perfect tool for doing this. But proper delegation is a demanding skill, not simply a way of reducing a manager's workload. Developing a team member from one who simply does as instructed, to one who takes responsibility for what to do, how to do it, and the actual accomplishment of tasks is a gradual process involving time, conscious effort and training.

Where team members are inexperienced or lack confidence or motivation, managers are often reluctant to delegate. The problem then is that staff will **not** develop and their lack of confidence and motivation is likely to be reinforced. And the manager is likely to be overworked and under pressure.

The manager aiming to motivate their staff and meet their growth needs will delegate **according to the experience and current abilities of staff** but will aim to **increase** the level of responsibility delegated as their experience, skills and confidence increase. Initially the manager's involvement in developmental delegation will certainly be high, but as staff become increasingly skilled, that involvement will correspondingly diminish.

Figure 6.2 shows how the **successive levels of delegation** may be used as **stages** by which the staff can grow in a controlled way in ability and self-confidence. Too often individual skills in a team lie undiscovered because such opportunities are not provided.

Levels of Delegation and Responsibility

Increasing Confidence of Supervisor in staff

	Stage 1	Stage 2	Stage 3	Stage 4
Manager level of delegation	Interpret goals	Interpret goals	Interpret goals	Interpret goals
	Specify results	Specify results	Specify results	Negotiate results
	What to do	What to do	What to do	What to do
	How to do	How to do	How to do	How to do
Staff level of responsibility	Do	Do	Do	Do

Increasing staff competence

fig 6.2

Supporting the Ladder

In climbing the ladder from stage to stage in responsibility levels, the staff are undertaking new tasks in which they need managerial support in terms of **access to time**, **materials**, and **equipment**. Equally crucial, however, is **personal support**.

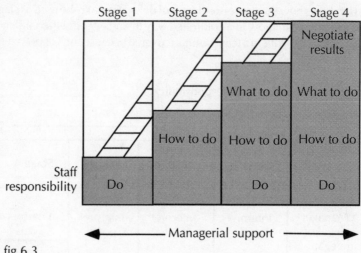

fig 6.3

A manager can 'hold the ladder' between stages by ensuring that

■ the chance of failure for the staff is relatively low. (No growth is possible without some risk of failure, but repeated failure is destructive for people)

■ more checkpoints than usual are in place so that, if the staff member does have trouble, back up can be provided in time to prevent serious problems for the organisation

■ the responsibility level and the level of risk are increased only gradually

■ the individual's strengths and weaknesses are known and considered in assigning work

■ encouragement and reassurance are given in the transitional period to show trust and develop their confidence and independence

There must also be proper discussion with the individual about the task being given to them.

ACTION POINT 31

What are the main points you think should be covered in 'proper discussion' of a delegated task?

Check your suggestions with the points which follow.

The manager will need to

Clearly indicate responsibility. Give an overview of the task in sufficient detail; state how the assignment must be done; explain the result required clearly and the time scale involved

Ensure understanding of the task. Check for understanding with open questions; explore the team member's plan of action and their awareness of resource centres

Check for possible problem areas. Discuss possible solutions, if necessary and establish checkpoints for monitoring, including a starting date

Ensure commitment. Check staff's readiness to undertake the assignment; indicate availability and support where required

ACTION POINT 32

Consider some of the areas where you have increased individual responsibility and discussed the setting of objectives with individuals in your work team. Have you noticed any difference in their attitude towards their work and how has this shown itself? If you felt any of your people were not as successful in taking on greater responsibility as you had hoped, can you identify the probable reasons for this?

Using Feedback to Motivate and Develop

We have mentioned feedback frequently as one of the essential managerial tools both in motivating individuals and in ensuring that teams keep on course in pursuing their work goals. You will doubtless be familiar with the general meaning of the term - and that in a work context it refers to **information** about performance that **leads to action** to change or maintain performance. However, it is important to realise that there are different types of feedback and that they should be used in different ways.

Motivational feedback tells a person that good performance has been noticed and gives recognition for it, so motivating them to repeat the good performance in the future.

Developmental feedback tells a person what needs to be done better and how to do it. Its purpose is to help the person perform better next time and so gain greater satisfaction.

To be most effective the two types should be

■ kept **separate** and not both given at the same time

■ given at **appropriate** times

ACTION POINT 33

Spend a few minutes thinking about why appropriate timing and separation of these two forms of feedback might be important. Jot down your thoughts.

Compare the points you have suggested with the paragraphs which follow.

Motivational feedback given **immediately after the performance** of some task will

■ reinforce the good performance with praise

■ allow the individual to gain confidence and to feel good about their job

Managers sometimes make the mistake of giving points of advice or suggestions for even better performance at the same time. Doing this is likely to negate the effect of the motivational feedback. **It will be seen as criticism** and a reflection on the team member's competence, so it is much better that this should be given at a different time.

Developmental feedback is best given **as advice just before the next performance** so that

■ the person is helped to do things better the next time (increasing their competence)

■ the feedback is seen as support rather than criticism

Of course there are occasions when reasons such as safety demand that developmental feedback is given immediately, but it should be given in a concerned and supportive manner rather than critically.

Look at the examples of both forms of feedback below.

Motivational feedback (immediately after performance)

'Chris, thanks for helping Mr Jones sort out that delivery problem just now - you really handled it well. I know just how tricky some of those situations can be, particularly when we are already under pressure.'

Developmental feedback (just before the next performance)

'Chris, tomorrow is going to be a busy day as you know and it's your turn to handle customer complaints and queries. Now last time we had some problems because you didn't complete the documentation properly and we had to trace the customers all over again. I know it's difficult when you are under pressure but try to give yourself more time to complete the paperwork and double check it before going on to the next job.'

Using Motivational Feedback

Positive feedback about good performance is most commonly given by direct **praise or 'strokes'** for good performance. This is very important for motivation; but publicising the success of an individual to others they respect will often give even greater satisfaction than direct praise and three effective ways of doing this are by

- **Earshot Praise** - by telling someone about a person's performance in a situation where they will overhear you

- **Third Party Recognition** - by encouraging someone else to compliment the individual for good performance

- **Formal Recognition** - by recommending them for reward or formal recognition

When recognition is given it is also important that it is not seen as automatic or mechanical or of no real significance. To be effective, as well as being correctly **timed**, recognition must be **focused** and it must **fit**.

Does it fit?

'Fit' means that the recognition is appropriate to the staff member and for the performance involved. Recognising a team member lavishly for a very simple task will come across as flattery or condescension. However, an off-hand 'Nice job', will hardly sound like genuine appreciation of outstanding effort on a project.

Is it focused?

'Focus' means making sure that the recognition is for a **specific performance** and that it is kept **separate** from any developmental feedback which may need to be given later.

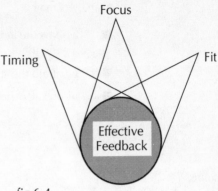

fig 6.4

Saying exactly what the good performance was identifies it for the individual and shows that the recognition is not just a fairly meaningless generality; keeping it separate from any other advice or suggestions will make sure it is effective as a motivator.

Using Developmental Feedback

Many managers tend to give formative or developmental feedback only at such times as performance reviews or appraisal; and as a result staff may justifiably complain that they did not realise they could be doing the job better, or how that could be achieved.

ACTION POINT 34

Why might managers fail to give regular developmental feedback?

Managers may

- assume the individual knows how to do the task but is simply not doing a good job

- be afraid the staff member will get upset or angry

- be unsure of how to give feedback effectively or unconvinced of its value

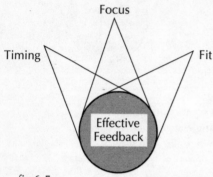

fig 6.5

But feedback - getting the reactions of others - is one of the major ways by which we **learn**, a very valuable tool for improving individual competence and achievement. And where people recognise from the way it is given that it is for the benefit of the job and their own performance, the common reactions of defensive denial or excuses and justification are likely to fade away.

Just as in giving motivational feedback, there are useful guidelines for giving helpful developmental feedback properly. They also relate to **fit, focus and timing**.

As we noticed earlier, for developmental feedback to be effective it must be given when it is most likely to be accepted, remembered and used - that is, just before the next performance of the task to be improved; but the other elements are also important.

Does it fit?

Is it the right kind of feedback for that particular person and situation? Fitness may include

(a) identifying the error - leaving choice of action to the individual

(b) suggesting corrective action, demonstrating personally, providing instruction

Is it focused?

Is the feedback focused

(a) on the behaviour not the person, avoiding personal criticisms of the individual?

(b) on the developmental issue - that is, not mixing the developmental with motivational feedback?

(c) on one subject at a time, at one person and without ambiguity?

ACTION POINT 35

Consider the following examples of poorly focused feedback. What do you think is wrong with each example? Write down your comments and say how you would put the feedback to improve it.

(a)   'John, you are a nuisance - you're always late for briefing'

(b)   'James, you're such a good worker but your reports are always a mess'

(c)   'Chris, will you make sure those figures are on my desk by 5 o'clock - oh, and can you help out with the new person while I'm out and make sure any visitors are looked after. It would have been a lot better for everyone if you had started on those figures earlier as I'd suggested . . .'

Developmental feedback used habitually can cover the full range of performance improvement - from correcting simple mistakes before they become habits to the most complex and involved work improvement and training discussions.

Its proper use involves

■   correcting work errors when they first occur before they become habitual or problematic

■   giving it in a non-threatening and matter of fact climate

■   describing the error, saying why it should be changed, suggesting what can be done, and expressing confidence that it will be corrected

■   checking that the person has understood and is committed to correcting the problem

Making Use of the Rewards Package

In looking at the development and motivation of individuals and teams - at what makes individuals and teams positive or dissatisfied, cohesive or disunited in their approach to work - we have concentrated so far on those elements which the manager or supervisor can most affect by their own actions and attitudes. But there are of course other very important influences which are under corporate control rather than that of individual managers.

ACTION POINT 36

What do you think are the primary motivating and developmental factors for individuals and team which are controlled by the organisation or **company** (leaving aside for the moment company training and education programmes)?

The other principal developmental and motivating factors under corporate rather than individual management control are

■　　pay and pay-linked incentives

■　　work design

With the framework set up by the organisation, managers have an important role to play in **understanding** how and why those policies are implemented, and in **being aware** of their part in implementing or monitoring them.

Work Design and Motivation

There are a number of different approaches to making work more rewarding and satisfying. But clearly the way tasks are arranged, co-ordinated and allocated must depend very much on

■　　the nature of the job itself

■　　the capabilities of those doing the work

Three common approaches are

- **job rotation** - organised on a formal basis where people rotate between different jobs

- **job enlargement** - by amalgamating a number of different tasks into a single job

- **job enrichment** - changing the job itself to make it more interesting to the individual

The first two have been found to make only small contributions to increasing job satisfaction, but may still be worthwhile. They seek to break work monotony and change the pace involved in the completion of a set of tasks. They are most effective motivationally if clearly seen by individuals as part of a targeted programme for individual growth.

If job rotation, for example, necessitates training in new skills which make a person better qualified for promotion or greater responsibilities, an individual could well respond with increased motivation.

Job enrichment offers more possibilities still. It is designed not simply to provide more variety but to give more responsibility, autonomy and control to people, satisfying their desires for growth and personal achievement. Its strategies include

- adding a variety of more complex tasks to a job over a period of time or giving the individual a whole piece of work to do

- providing more developmental feedback and giving individuals specific tasks so that they are able to become experts in these activities

- removing some of the controls and supervision and increasing the level of responsibility for the job

Job Enrichment in Practice

Many companies have attempted job enrichment exercises. In the early stages of a programme at ICI it was found that though sales reps felt increased job satisfaction, the company had shown no improvement in its sales. Further changes were then made so that

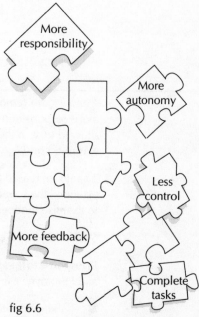

fig 6.6

1   Sales reps no longer had to report on every customer call, but simply to pass on information they thought useful and request action if they thought it was required

2   Responsibility for determining when to call on customers was placed entirely with the representatives themselves

3   If customers complained about product performance, representatives could now make immediate settlement of up to £100 if they judged it appropriate

4   If material was faulty, or if customers had material they had no further use for, the rep was given complete authority to decide how to deal with the situation

5   They were given a discretionary range of about 10% on the prices of most products, with the lower limit often below any price previously quoted in the sales office

---

ACTION POINT 37

A job enrichment programme attempts to strengthen or introduce certain **motivators** in the work. For each change in the ICI enrichment programme, note at least one motivational factor which is introduced.

---

1 and 2 both removed some of the previous controls and gave the salesmen more responsibility, autonomy and scope for initiative. The changes also showed trust in their judgement and recognition of their capacity to do what was necessary.

3 again increased the level of responsibility exercise in the job and, like 4, it extended the scope of their job, providing greater challenge through the need to exercise independent, responsible judgement.

5 again removed controls and gave greater freedom of action and decisions.

In response to these changes, Paul and Robertson (in their book 'Job Enrichment and Employee Motivation') report that

■   the job satisfaction of the salesmen further increased

- customers felt they were dealing with more responsible representatives
- sales increased and complaints were dealt with more quickly

It is important to note that the changes were 'enabling' ones, allowing an individual, personal response from each employee concerned. As a result, those who wished to exercise more responsibility and control were able to, whilst those who did not wish to take on that extra responsibility did not feel pressured to.

Job Enrichment and Autonomous Groups

Another approach to job enrichment is centred around the structure of working groups and the **relationship** between members of those groups.

Autonomous Working Groups, for example, are small units of people who are given

- responsibility for a whole task
- a good deal of autonomy in deciding how to carry it out

Individuals within the group have some degree of **choice** as to the number of tasks they perform and may extend their skills in different areas of the work over the work performance time. Rewards are linked to the performance of the total group, rather than to individual performance, recognising the dynamic effect of group loyalty and teamwork as a powerful factor in individual motivation and development.

Where the responsibility of the group is increased gradually evidence shows that people are willing and able to accept it. Where they operate successfully the motivation of team individuals is increased as they find

- closer and stronger work relationships
- greater challenge and fulfilment in the work

Pay and Pay-linked Incentives

Although we have seen that people work for more than just money, pay is obviously a prime motivational factor if only because

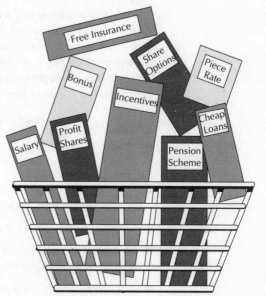

fig 6.7

■ it allows us to purchase much that will satisfy our needs

■ it is symbolic of recognition and achievement

'Pay' as a motivator is also more complex than just the wage or salary notified on a pay slip. There is a whole group of money-related or valuable rewards for working, which are referred to as **The Rewards Package**.

ACTION POINT 38

Which elements do you feel are part of your 'Rewards Package'?

Wages and Salaries

Whatever else there is in a rewards package, the basic salary is in most cases the most important element of it. Where total gross salary is actually related to performance (through a personal or team-based incentive scheme) it can be a positive motivator as well. Certainly where the salary is inadequate or the salary structure is not well thought out, it can be (to use Herzberg's terms) a potent 'dissatisfier' or 'demotivator.'

A good salary system will need to be

■ fair compared with outside bodies, and therefore sufficient to keep staff from leaving

■ consistent internally, so that higher-valued jobs attract a higher salary, and similar jobs the same salary

■ flexible enough to handle unusual or unique jobs

■ subject to negotiation by the union, staff body or individuals, or on appeal against injustices

■ consistent with the economic environment, so that it allows for inflation or changing economic circumstances

Financial Incentives and 'Perks'

These could be extremely wide ranging in both amount and the criteria used for allocating them. They could include

- annual bonus (based on corporate or branch targets)

- profit sharing (on a similar basis)

- annual, monthly or weekly bonuses and incentives (based on individual or team targets)

- share options or allocations, loans, health insurance, non contributory pensions and so on

While details of such incentives will be available through personnel channels and company notices, most staff look to their supervisors or managers to explain and clarify the schemes to them. So managers need to have a clear grasp of what benefits of this type are in operation, who is eligible for them, what they may be worth to individuals or teams, on what basis they are allocated, how they are obtained and so on. The company 'rewards package' will not be a very powerful motivator for team or individuals if staff are uncertain what is available and how it may be obtained.

ACTION POINT 39

Check on your own awareness of the detail of any financial incentive or rewards schemes operating within your department or company. If you are in doubt about any aspects of them, find out the necessary information.

CHAPTER SUMMARY

Having completed this chapter, you should now

- understand the role of delegation and feedback in developing individuals and teams and be able to use them effectively

- realise the need to recognise the feelings generated between team members and encourage openness

If you are uncertain about any of these areas, look back and re-read the relevant parts of the text.

7 USING OBJECTIVES FOR WORK ACHIEVEMENT

All the factors we have looked at which contribute to team cohesion and individual development will not create an achieving team without the establishment of a clear direction and purpose - a common enterprise - which all understand and are committed to. Without clear and relevant aims and goals, motivation and effort result in activity which is haphazard, wasteful and unproductive. **Relevant, achievable objectives** are the basis of any meaningful planning since they make us

- define our aims
- focus upon the purpose of what we are doing
- relate all our activities to the results we want

An approach to work planning through objectives will be concerned with four principal activities

- identifying within a team or section or department those areas which need priority attention to contribute best to overall **company goals** and to achieve **specific work goals** successfully

- setting (and monitoring) performance targets and objectives in each area which will keep individuals on course to achieve the goals successfully

- measuring performance to see whether what we set out to achieve is accomplished

- using the results of monitoring by feedback to tell people what they have achieved and set new goals, or to assess why goals were not achieved, take action to ensure future success and so on

Identify Key Areas for Success

Performance Set Goals

Monitor Progress Measure Performance

Give feedback Review success

fig 7.1

ACTION POINT 40

Jot down what you see as the basic essential processes involved in planning successful work achievement through the use of objectives.

Identifying Key Areas

Identifying the key areas in which objectives must be met if goals are to be achieved has always to be seen in the context of overall company aims. If the company aim is to be a market leader in a type of laser printer for example, that may at times have to override cost and pricing considerations which might normally dictate the objectives and actions of the Finance Department.

Corporate Objectives

These overall aims will be the company's **Corporate Objectives** and they are the aims to which all the activities of its different departments should contribute. They will define the long-term objectives as well as the shorter term goals of a company - where it sees itself going in terms of such things as markets, product and service development, the percentage level of growth or profitability to be reached over a particular period and so on.

A major airline corporate objective might be, for example - 'To at least match the annual total growth of the world airline market.'

Departmental, Sectional and Individual Objectives

These will cover

- actions needed now to move towards longer term objectives
- goals for reaching specific results in the day-to-day running of any department

Departments identify key areas of activity and agree the objectives within them which will need to be met to achieve corporate goals. (In the example we took above, a marketing department objective to support corporate goals might be 'To achieve a 5% increase in long haul passenger sales over a 12 month period'). Then, within each department, similar key areas and targets are agreed for every unit or section - so that every unit's work will support the department's objectives. And finally, within the unit, key areas and targets are identified and agreed for individuals, so that the unit's goals will be achieved.

As when we looked at company structure, we find here a 'Pyramid' effect, with increasing numbers of objectives at every lower level, but all directed towards supporting the corporate goals. Each individual, each section and department pursuing their targets of achievement can then relate them to the company's aims and will be part of a cohesive overall company strategy.

In addition to ensuring consistent and purposeful co-ordination of planning, effort and activities (for both the long and short terms), setting objectives has an important **motivational value** since individuals have a clearer sense of purpose and direction, and of how their work fits into the larger context. They are also an important way of bringing about **continuous improvement** and development in work **achievement** and aspirations.

Setting Objectives

Deciding on particular work objectives will, of course, also require **analysis of the area of work** to see what are the critical areas of performance that will decide whether work goals are achieved. Achieving ever higher standards in some area of marginal importance to the main work goals is not simply pointless; it is a wasteful distraction.

When key issues for success have been identified, the process of setting objectives follows. In discussing or deciding on the criteria which will be used to measure success it is always important to **ask 'the customer'** who will be receiving your product or service what the criteria are which will satisfy them. The 'customer' may be someone in your own company - your manager, someone in another department affected by your work, other colleagues etc - who require things of you, or it may be a customer in the literal sense outside your own organisation.

Generally speaking the success criteria for objectives will be expressed in terms of

- ■ 'customer' needs (frequency, quality, quantity, accuracy, detail etc)
- ■ constraints (timescale allowed, costs, resource limits etc)

These will then be the basis for measuring progress and performance in the key areas of work - but they should not be regarded as being rigid and non-negotiable, for when progress is reviewed in any particular area it may be appropriate to revise the criteria according to changing circumstances and constraints.

In some companies managers or supervisors essentially decide these and pass them on to their teams. Companies where a **shared contribution and discussion** are encouraged before objectives are set believe that they are then more likely to be achievable and achieved. Where all in a department, or a unit or work team, can involve themselves in the objectives at these different levels, there is likely to be a **greater motivation and commitment** to achieving them, as people can identify themselves with the decisions.

The aims are also likely then to be **more realistic** and **more imaginative**, since the people concerned with their setting are familiar with the work, know the problems, and can contribute to solutions. This is important for success since setting unrealistic targets is a sure recipe for failure and demoralisation.

Even if objectives are not evolved through discussion, at the very least they should be **explained clearly** and **agreed** with everyone involved in meeting them.

Writing Objectives

Well formulated objectives should

■   be written down in clear, **unambiguous** language

■   be **specific** in defining the area of responsibility referred to and the result to be produced

■   define a **quantitative** goal wherever possible and aim for **measurable** results

■   be keyed to a **given time** schedule

■   be established in all **key areas** for achieving team, section or department goals

To make clear what that means, let's continue the airline example.

A particular manager's responsibilities there fall into a number of functional areas: Administration, Personnel, Finance, Customer Contact, Production and Technical. And within each there may be areas which will be relevant and important to the airline's corporate goals and the departmental goals which support them. If we look at her duties in Customer Contact, for example, she may be responsible for

(a)   passenger acceptance and check in

(b)   receipt and proper labelling of customer baggage

(c)   producing a customer list for the flight captain, and so on.

For each of the key areas she should have an agreed, specified goal against which to define the standard of performance she is expected to achieve. Taking item (b), for example, the standard of performance or objective might be expressed as 'To achieve a 98.5% accuracy in the labelling of customer baggage for every flight during the next year.'

There she has a **quantitative** aim (98.5%) for a **specific** area (all flights) related to a **given time** schedule (the next year); and the achievement, or progress towards it, is **measurable** at the end of that year.

Sometimes objectives refer to standards of **quality** instead of measurable quantities - 'To improve customer service', for example. It is not possible to measure performance for objectives expressed in this way (however desirable), but with a little thought most objectives can be made more specific and quantitative - in this case by stating it as 'To reduce the number of customer complaints on my section by 50% over the next 3 months'.

ACTION POINT 41

If you have not already got a set of agreed work objectives yourself, identify a specific area of work responsibility in your own work which is a key area in achieving section or departmental work goals. Write down a major goal which you are expected to achieve in that area and the standards of performance which could be used to measure your level of achievement in that area. Do this for each area of your responsibilities.

Go through the standards of performance you have written down (or those given in your actual work objectives) and check each one to see if it contains a quantitative measure, a time schedule, a specific description and an achievable objective.

Timescales are particularly important in setting out objectives where these relate to specific tasks and projects which are underway and are tied into **schedules**. Breaking down a job into stages or components and setting realistic target dates for their completion - targets which will **allow for review and adaptation** where necessary - are essential parts of achieving work goals successfully.

Using Objectives Successfully

A final critical part of using objectives successfully is the monitoring of performance and progress once set - particularly as we have just noted, where production or other schedules are involved also. Whether in relation to an individual's goals and work performance or to team progress towards joint work goals, appropriate monitoring is essential in the form of work progress reviews or individual performance reviews, to give the opportunity to

- identify and resolve problems

- modify goals or bring in additional resources to achieve them

- ensure both individuals and team keep on course

- motivate to continued effort

- give feedback about progress and performance

- give praise or work improvement counselling, or arrange instruction or training where appropriate

- re-discuss the goals or targets and clear up any misunderstandings by mutual agreement

The reviews might be at monthly or three monthly or six monthly intervals, depending upon the particular tasks involved to get the desired results. Success will be judged in a final review stage, by measuring the **actual outputs** against the outcomes we had **aimed for**.

Using Objectives for Development

Our discussion of objectives so far has been related very much to task goals achievement. But there are other areas in which the use of objectives can be of great value to the manager and team.

ACTION POINT 42

Can you suggest what these other areas might be?

As well as ongoing job requirements - the kind of activities we might call 'operational' - objectives may be used in such areas as

■ special assignments or projects of limited span and arising from particular circumstances

■ staff development - in such areas as skills training or delegated responsibility or personal development, as part of a planned programme of personal growth and motivation for staff

■ self development - setting goals for yourself over periods of time to develop your own knowledge, skills, personal growth and so on

One of the most important aspects of objectives for performance management is that the monitoring enables you to identify the 'gaps' between performance and aspiration. And this is one of the vital elements of identifying **training or coaching needs** as we shall see in the next section of the book.

In addition to setting goals for performance generally and identifying goals to remedy weaker performance, we can also use objectives to set goals for continuous improvement of performance in cases where the standards initially reached leave further improvements still possible.

Diagrammatically, the use of objectives to manage performance in this way might be shown as in figure 7.2 .

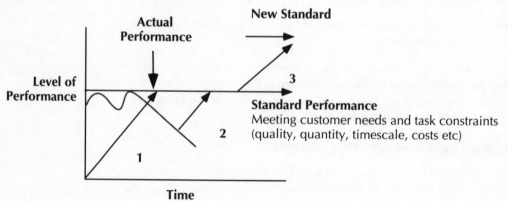

fig 7.2

Actual performance will usually appear like the path of the dotted line - above or below the standard we are aiming for. In the diagram

(1)   represents a key result for an inexperienced team member aiming for that standard

(2)   would be a key result target set to remedy lower than acceptable performance

(3)   represents a change in the objective standard itself in the search for even better performance

---

ACTION POINT 43

During your study of this section you wrote objectives and performance standards for one of your areas of responsibility.

Take all your other areas of responsibility in turn and write clear and unambiguous objectives for each one, and standards of performance which meet the requirements that they should be 'results orientated, quantitative and measurable'.

CHAPTER SUMMARY

Having completed this chapter, you should now

- ■   recognise the central importance of objectives for goal achievement and team development and be able to formulate, use and monitor them

- ■   understand the factors which build cohesive teams and know how to manage team roles

If you are uncertain about any of these areas, look back and re-read the relevant parts of the text.

8 CONSTRAINTS ON TEAM PERFORMANCE

No matter how successful the manager or supervisor is in building a team and motivating their people, and no matter how effectively they use objectives to focus on work goals and manage performance, there will be constraints from both within the team and outside it which will affect team performance and within which they will have to work.

ACTION POINT 44

Make two lists noting down examples of any internal and external constraints you can think of which could affect team performance.

Within the team the **abilities, experience, skills, task maturity and motivations** of individuals are constraints which the manager will have to work with, even at the same time as they may try to stretch these by encouraging their development and commitment in every way they can. In the same way **current team relationships and roles**, including any 'gaps' there may be, have to be worked with **as they are** even whilst the supervisor or manager tries to influence the team towards an ideal cohesiveness of morale and purpose.

Externally the team may be limited in what it can achieve by such things as

- the equipment, staffing and resources which are available
- organisational structures and procedures as we noted earlier
- the timescales within which work must be done
- cost limits in labour, materials and production processes
- dependence on other departments, outside suppliers, contractors or consultants
- customer specifications or needs

and so on.

There will also be **areas of uncertainty** which will be outside the immediate control of the team and the manager, but for which decisions and activities cannot be held up, so that they carry the possibility of less than the best achievement in the final outcomes.

How should the manager and team respond to such constraints to perform still in the most effective manner?

ACTION POINT 45

Note down briefly any ideas you have on how these constraints and uncertainties should be approached.

The most important points to remember are that the manager or supervisor should

- **recognise** the areas of constraints and uncertainty
- distinguish clearly between those areas they **can** do something about and those they **cannot**
- do whatever they can to limit their effect on the team's performance in the immediate future and in the longer term
- accept those they cannot alter and **take them realistically** into account in planning and scheduling processes, and in setting objectives and work goals

Doing something about modifiable constraints or areas of uncertainty may involve all sorts of activities - training, restructuring, negotiating longer 'lead' times, seeking further information, considering a range of possible outcomes, taking up questions at a later date and so on.

Taking them into account in planning and setting objectives means being realistic about what actual team resources can achieve in the particular circumstances, balancing the aim of the best possible performance against the constraints you will be working under and the possible effects if uncertain factors prove detrimental. It may well also involve **contingency planning** where there is uncertainty - that is, planning to meet a number of possible outcomes. (It is easy though to overplan for contingencies as we shall see when we look at work planning and scheduling processes in a later part of this book).

To take on unrealistic goals - either through pressure from others or perfectionism in oneself - and to plan for some ideal outcome ignoring constraints and uncertainties is to invite failure. It is also likely to put both team and manager under intolerable and demoralising pressures.

CHAPTER SUMMARY

Having completed this chapter, you should now

- understand the need to recognise areas of constraints and uncertainty and do whatever you can to limit their effect on the team's performance

- realise the importance of using contingency planning where there is uncertainty, to meet a number of possible outcomes

If you are uncertain about any of these areas, look back and re-read the relevant parts of the text.

9 SELF MANAGEMENT FOR WORK ACHIEVEMENT

Research suggests that the majority of supervisors and managers spend only about 30-40% of their time upon the most important and essential elements of their job. It also indicates that there is a high incidence of work stress experienced among these staff groups.

If you think back to a competitive sport you have engaged in, or a short-term overload of work you have coped with, you will probably agree that **pressure** can be the cause of good performance. Working for short periods to achieve good results in a limited time can galvanise us into energetic and productive action with a flow of adrenalin that makes us feel good - even 'at our best'.

On the other hand, too much pressure over a period of time tends to produce **stress** with a loss of effectiveness - a sapping of concentration, judgement, energy, and confidence in which work takes longer to produce and is often inefficiently done. Consciousness of these problems may become an additional stress factor also, so that the more stressed a person is, the more stressful their situation becomes.

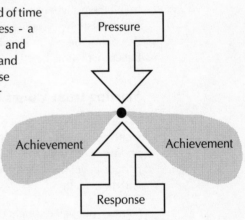

fig 9.1

In more acute situations stress may well show itself in

- physical symptoms (agitation, shallow breathing, increased muscular tension, headaches, loss of energy and vitality, high blood pressure, ulcers, strokes or heart attacks)

- mental or behavioural symptoms (inability to relax, insomnia, depression, distortion of judgement, nervous agitation - and in extreme cases, mental confusion and nervous breakdown)

Such problems highlight the importance of the self management skills in someone responsible for achieving results through other people. Management responsibility already brings with it the stress of working with many factors over which we have limited or no control. But by taking conscious thought about their own temperament, priorities, responsibilities and behaviour managers can do much to

- minimise the risk of suffering stress
- be more effective in their own performance

First of all managers need to recognise that many causes of stress may be within their own power to control - such things as

- not taking time for recreation and relaxation
- losing sight of the overall goals and context of work activities
- failing to plan and prioritise effectively
- taking on unreasonable tasks and responsibilities and other people's problems
- inefficient use of available time and procrastination over difficult problems
- poor communications

Secondly, the manager needs to develop a fundamental and consistent strategy to put themselves in control of their management of time, stress and pressure; and that strategy should begin from their own personal needs and values. Beginning there is in the organisation's interest too, since work goals will be better met with a healthy, effective and unstressed manager.

Starting from Values

Values are an expression of our needs. They are the ends which we feel are worth pursuing for their own sake. Those we hold and the importance we place on individual ones may be widely varied, and they may change at different periods in our lives, as you will remember from our earlier discussion of needs and motivation.

Some of our values might be

- to be financially secure, have a comfortable home and be happy in our family life
- to develop our intellectual and creative abilities
- to relate well to others
- to achieve power or status or recognition at work
- to have the time and resources needed for our leisure interests

and so on.

ACTION POINT 46

What are **your** values?

However different people's values may be in detail, it seems likely that most people would aim

- to be happy in their work and home life

- to have good physical and mental health

- to be effective in their life and in their career

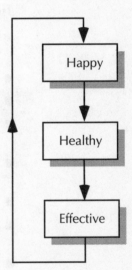

fig 9.2

Of course there are factors over which we have not total control (physical health, for instance) but for managers who share those values, they have clear implications for their general **approach to work**.

Amongst other things, they will consciously

- plan their life and work, so that they have an underlying sense of being reasonably in control of events rather than constantly harassed by problems

- lead a balanced life and place conscious and realistic limits on their work involvement so that they have time for family and friends and the recreation which will refresh them and keep them in good health. Workaholics are generally not effective

- set high but realistic standards, avoiding the pressures of 'perfectionism'

- distinguish clearly between what is possible and what is impossible, and learn to say 'No' to unreasonable demands and pressures

- learn not to be over dependent on the goodwill and approval of others (which may be withdrawn at times of disagreement)

- take reasonable breaks during the working day to refresh themselves

■ confront difficult issues without procrastination. Every 'live' problem ticking away in the 'Pending' tray is a source of stress and a drain on energy reserves

■ accept occasional failures as inevitable and as opportunities for learning and developing, not as reflections upon their personal worth which cause stress and demoralisation

Most of these things are to do with managers consciously adopting a balanced mental attitude to work which respect their own rights and values, but in the sphere of time management and planning particularly there are a number of **specific techniques** which the manager can use.

Time Management Techniques

In brief the kinds of time management aids which will help the manager avoid stress and be more effective are to

■ plan the day's work and set priorities

■ work to agreed and realistic deadlines

■ plan their office and desk to minimise clutter, time-wasting and interruptions

■ use delegation and shelving of work where appropriate work and review the tasks as necessary periodically

■ keep paperwork and records under control

■ manage your conversations, telephone calls and meetings efficiently and eliminate time wasting

■ support your team, but encourage them to own their own problems

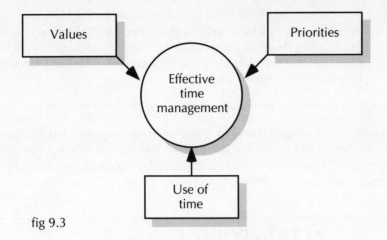

fig 9.3

We shall look at ways of doing these things in the chapter which follows.

Encouraging Others to Own their own Problems

Do not let your staff convert **their** problems into **your** problems.

When team members come with **their** work problems and you **accept full responsibility** for the next stage in solving the problem, you have taken on more pressure.

Oncken and Wass in a Harvard Business Review article (1974), memorably described this kind of reverse delegation as 'passing the monkey'. A team member has a problem which is a worry or burden like 'a monkey on his or her back'. The person comes to see the manager, who discovers that somehow when the person goes away, the monkey stays behind and is now on their back!

Feeding other people's monkeys is bad self management. It is also bad for team members themselves who then exercise less responsibility and initiative and stop 'owning' their problems as a matter of course. It is not the way to develop a team into motivated, successful individuals who have confidence in themselves and high self esteem.

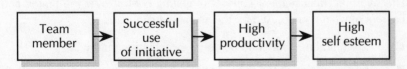

fig 9.4

Though a manager is ultimately responsible for achieving team goals and people need to know they have managerial support, it should also be clear that wherever possible, they take suitable action themselves and report what they have done. And that if they do have to bring a problem, they are expected to bring with it their suggestions for a solution.

Managers should also discourage the reporting of problems by memo.

It is all too easy for such problems to end up on the manager's desk. You might want a written report on a problem for your **information** only, but emphasise that you want staff to report problems face-to-face or by telephone - and with suggested solutions.

ACTION POINT 47

1   Count the number of jobs which are 'pending' on your desk.

2   Now make two lists out of this work: one for 'monkeys' and one for your own work.

3   Count the number of 'monkeys' you have in hand.

4   Make a few notes on how you will return any 'monkeys' you are harbouring to their rightful owners.

Setting Priorities

Effective time management consists of getting control over the timing and content of what you do. And for the manager that means

■   concentrating your effort on your key activities, not trivia

■   delegating urgent tasks that do not require your personal involvement

■   shelving any activities which are neither vital nor urgent

Four levels of priority might be used once work tasks have been identified

A   =   I **must** do this (It's vital, it's my work, it's urgent)

B   =   I **should** do this (It's vital, it's my work, but **not** urgent)

C   =   I **could** do this (It's not vital and it's not urgent)

D   =   **Delegate this** now (It's not vital, but it is urgent)

fig 9.5

Vital tasks would be those of **central importance** to achieving departmental or unit work goals. Urgency relates to the **timescale** in which a task must be done. As time passes things become more urgent, but they do not become any more important than they always were.

ACTION POINT 48

1   Make a diary log sheet for your **activities** at half-hourly intervals for a whole week. Read through that list now and put an A, B, C or D next to each activity.

2   Now count up the total number of tasks undertaken between Monday and Friday, as recorded on the diary log sheet. Then the total number of 'A's you recorded from Monday to Friday.

3   What percentage of your time did you spend on key activities ('A's)?

4   What does that tell you about your use of time?

Most people who do this exercise find that they spend between 10 and 30% of their time on key activities and 70 to 90% on non-vital tasks which could have been delegated or even shelved. Effective time management demands a decisive shift to spending more time on key activities.

A useful way of classifying activities to help people prioritise and delegate appropriately is to identify where an activity would fall on the following simple chart.

	Very Important	Not Important
Very Urgent	A	D
Not Urgent	B	C

If a task is both very important and very urgent ('A'), it should get top priority attention. All 'B' and 'C' tasks can wait, while 'D' tasks should be delegated. The approach can get rid of as much as 80% of the pressure on the manager, and free time for priority 'A' tasks and vital activities which require discretionary time such as leadership, identifying opportunities and giving careful thought to the 'B' tasks.

'B' and 'C' tasks should be out of sight for the **immediate** present, but reviewed and re-prioritised from time to time.

The danger with 'B' type jobs (which may have no deadline or where the deadline is a fair time in the future) is that they may not be tackled until they become 'A' priority jobs or crises. But because 'B' type tasks are important for the long term success and goals of a team, they should be reviewed and planned for as and when 'A' type tasks have been dealt with.

It is easy to spend too much managerial time on type 'D' tasks instead of standing back and delegating them for urgent completion by someone else competent to take them on.

Planning and Organising Your Time

In many areas of work day to day operational constraints will affect the organisation and use of your working time to a considerable degree, but any supervisory or managerial job can be more effectively performed if we

■   use daily planning to concentrate on priorities

■   organise paperwork and records effectively

■   eliminate or reduce time-wasting activity

Daily Planning

A simple way of ensuring we prioritise each day is to work from a daily plan like that given below, instead of from a jumbled list, or tackling things as they come to mind, or appear on the desktop. Adapting such a form for personal use will give the manager a clear picture at a glance of how their work plan is progressing.

Day:			
Date:			
	Task Details	Time/Deadline	Delegation To
Urgent Phone Calls			
Must Be Done			
Should Be Done			
Could Be Done			
Future Reference, Notes etc			

ACTION POINT 49

If you do not already plan your time in a similar manner, prepare and use over the next week a daily planning sheet adapted for your job from this model. Note down your comments during the week about its effect and usefulness.

Keeping Records and Paperwork under Control

Simple record sheets or file cards are easily created, which give information quickly and ensure that approaching deadlines or checkdates are not missed in areas like Task Delegation, Individual Staff Development and Training records, or the analysis and monitoring of specific work tasks and projects.

A manager might, for example, draw up a simple **Project or Task Chart** analysing all the things which needed to be done to reach a particular goal. You could then identify

- which steps would require preliminary decisions to be taken

- what inputs in the way of resources, people etc were required

- what order the different stages should follow (using a flow chart if necessary)

- which parts of the task might be worked on simultaneously

- a timetable for implementing and 'dovetailing' the various activities efficiently

And to monitor progress effectively where several people are involved in different aspects of a project, a chart showing the division of responsibilities, with check dates and deadlines for each individual's work, would help ensure that target dates are kept.

It is important, however, that records like this are not over-elaborate and are **worthwhile**. The manager needs to weigh up the time needed for them against their usefulness in keeping the team on target, and against the time saved in streamlining a task and keeping track of its progress.

ACTION POINT 50

Consider whether you could improve your own organising and monitoring of your team's work or personal development by preparing some **simple** card index or record sheets on the lines described (if you do not already do so). Assess the benefits against the time that they would involve. Draw up any you consider would make you more effective in managing your time and in your supervision generally.

Other ways for the manager to avoid paperwork piling up include

■ taking decisions immediately, wherever possible. A memo or problem going into the 'Pending' file, means it has to be read and thought about **again** later. Unless further information is needed, a decision will be no better for the delay and there will be less time to put it right, if it is wrong

■ if something cannot be dealt with immediately, making marginal notes made on first reading will save time later

■ replying by phone, where feasible, to save time and expense in preparing letters, memos etc

■ discouraging 'For Information' copies or written memos unless the supervisor or manager really needs to see them

■ checking that returns or reports being submitted are actually used and that the information cannot be passed in any other way

■ setting aside a regular uninterrupted time for routine daily paperwork

Eliminating Time Wasters

There are many ways in which we waste time each day and effective time management demands that we identify and take action to eliminate them.

ACTION POINT 51

Note some ways in which you find time is wasted during a working day.

We have already mentioned delay in tackling difficult tasks and team members bringing problems they could deal with themselves. You may also have mentioned such things as

■ over-long or unnecessary conversations on the phone or face to face

■ 'drop in' visitors

■ unnecessary or poorly chaired meetings without clear agendas

■ indecision on difficult evaluations or priorities

■ excessive time spent reading or drafting documents

■ poor communication causing confusion and repetition

The importance of good communication and decision making for team performance are points we shall look at separately but in **all** these areas skills and techniques to reduce time wasting can be practised and developed.

Managing a Conversation

Apart from the casual, social and personal conversations with which managers help to create a good team climate and good relations with team colleagues, conversations should be kept as clear and to the point as possible. This is helped if the individual

■ is clear about their purpose and what needs saying, leaving out unnecessary detail

■ organises their thoughts logically first and thinks about how best to get over important information effectively

■ summarises where necessary to ensure first time understanding

Listening skills are also needed to manage conversation effectively

■ giving complete attention and listening for essentials, not chasing peripheral details

■ checking understanding as necessary and where a speaker rambles, guiding them back to the subject politely

■ making notes where the subject is complex to save time later

■ discussing what is said where necessary, but avoiding personalised argument

Managing a Phone Conversation

By taking similar care to have clear objectives and ordered thoughts before you make a phone call, phone time may be reduced considerably, as well as by very simple expedients like

■ keeping frequently used numbers visible by the phone with a note pad and pen

■ identifying yourself immediately to avoid unnecessary questions and delay

■ letting the caller know it will be a quick call following the TEA pattern

Tell the person, in a sentence if possible, your purpose in calling

Explain briefly the material information or questions

Activate by saying what you plan to do or what you want the person to do

■ where a person is out, getting a specific call back time to reach them, not trying 'on spec' or waiting for them to phone back

Meetings and Time Management

Poorly handled and unnecessary meetings cause much lost time (and hence pressure) for managers.

Whether it is a performance review, a problem solving discussion, a briefing session or any other gathering, time will be used much more productively where

■ there is a good reason for the meeting and the objectives for it will be best served by a meeting of that type (A meeting of 12 people to discuss punctuality because two staff are regularly late is not time efficient - or good for team morale)

■ an agenda is used, the need for each item is considered beforehand and discussion is kept to it

■ a time limit is set (preferably for each agenda item) and it is stuck to

■ attendance is limited to the people really needed for dealing with agenda items

■ the reasons for the meeting and the outcomes sought are made clear to participants in time for all material and ideas to be properly prepared

■ aids are set up in advance and the meeting begins on time, whether or not everyone is present

■ discussion is kept moving by relevant questioning, by summarising progress or different views succinctly at appropriate points and by moving the discussion tactfully onwards

---

ACTION POINT 52

Look back to the last Action Point. Take the 3 main time wasters you had written down and make notes on what could be done to eliminate each. Suggest a time span and deadline for putting them into operation.

By developing self management and time management skills, the manager will not only maintain their own personal health and performance; they may also have an important effect by example and by demonstration of the skills, on the attitude of team individuals towards managing themselves and on their abilities to do so effectively.

CHAPTER SUMMARY

Having completed this chapter, you should now

■ be able to manage your time, your tasks and yourself effectively and avoid excessive stress

■ understand the importance of a written record of progress and an account of the division of responsibilities

■ realise the necessity for good communication and be aware of the skills involved in managing a conversation

If you are uncertain about any of these areas, look back and re-read the relevant parts of the text.